Carmela Sophia Sereno, an Italian food writer and cookery tutor, was brought up on a small farm in the north of Bedfordshire. Though she was raised on the outskirts of Bedford town, known by many as 'Little Italy', her family originates from the regions of Puglia and Molise in the south of Italy. Today, Carmela lives in a small Northamptonshire village with her four children and husband, where she balances family life with her work as an Italian food writer, cookery tutor, chef, demonstrator and recipe developer.

Carmela shares her love of Italian food through her work as an Italian cookery author, magazine contributor and fortnightly food columnist for local newspaper *The Chronicle & Echo*. Her writing has brought her to the attention of Filippo Berio, who sponsor her fortnightly supper club, the success of which sees each session sold out months in advance.

Carmela's first book, *Southern Italian Family Cooking*, was a true labour of love, which showcased the best dishes of Southern Italy. The recipes in this book show her passion for the *cucina povera* style of cooking and encourage the use of seasonal ingredients in everyday family cooking. Carmela's second book, *A Passion for Pasta*, showcases different regional pastas alongside their complementary sauces.

For more details, please visit www.carmelas-kitchen.com

Happy Italian cooking!
love Penny 2020

Also by Carmela Sophia Sereno

Southern Italian Family Cooking
A Passion for Pasta

Northern & Central Italian Family Cooking
Italian Dishes for the Seasonal Kitchen

Carmela Sophia Sereno

A How To Book

ROBINSON

ROBINSON

First published in Great Britain in
2020 by Robinson

10 9 8 7 6 5 4 3 2 1

Copyright © Carmela Sophia Sereno,
2020

A CIP catalogue record for this book
is available from the British Library.

ISBN: 978-1-47214-413-3

Typeset in Great Britain by
Mousemat Design Limited

Printed and bound in Great Britain by
Clays Ltd, Elcograf S.p.A.

Papers used by Robinson are from
well-managed forests and other
responsible sources.

MIX
Paper from
responsible sources
FSC
www.fsc.org FSC® C104740

Robinson
An imprint of
Little, Brown Book Group
Carmelite House
50 Victoria Embankment
London EC4Y 0DZ

An Hachette UK Company
www.hachette.co.uk

www.littlebrown.co.uk

How To Books are published by
Robinson, an imprint of Little,
Brown Book Group. We welcome
proposals from authors who have
first-hand experience of their
subjects. Please set out the aims
of your book, its target market and
its suggested contents in an email
to howto@littlebrown.co.uk

My third cookery book is dedicated to the head of our family,
Nonna Carmela Sereno,
now ninety years old and forever my inspiration.

Ti amo sempre, I love you forever. La tua prima nipotina,
your eldest granddaughter Carmela xx

Contents

Introduction – 'Inspire me'

My eldest son calls me most days on his way home from college, or he'll sometimes drop me a text mid-afternoon. He asks the same question every day: 'What's for dinner, Mum?' and I love receiving this call. I want to please his hunger. Sometimes I win and sometimes I fail miserably.

I remember doing the same when I was seventeen and on the bus home from college. I'd phone my mum and start quizzing her about what was for dinner. Mum would always cook fresh wholesome food, as it's fair to say my father Rocco is a little fussy – sorry, Pops! If Mum hadn't made it from scratch, then Dad wouldn't eat it. I remember the time Mum bought posh (loosely speaking) supermarket meatballs and tried to pass them off as her own in her homemade tomato sugo (sauce), just in the spirit of saving a little time. Let's just say she never did it again and we still laugh about it now.

Most of the time I was happy with what Mum was cooking for dinner, as she is an exceptional cook, but on the odd occasion she would incorporate mushrooms. I can't begin to tell you how much I hated the autumnal slippery little suckers. I remember them having a slimy, almost slug-like texture. I would tell Mum, 'If I eat them, I'll be certain to die.' I can still hear Mum screaming down the phone at me. Guess what, I didn't die and I no longer refer to the humble, versatile mushroom as a slug; in fact, I love them!

A question for you: where do you get your inspiration to cook? Where is the inspiration that urges you to cook, the inspiration that encourages the chef in you to explore your larder or pantry? What inspires you to search out the freshest vine tomatoes or the most delicious cured meat? Is it a person, a place, a memory, or something else?

I am always inspired to cook by and for my family. In all fairness, I have no choice; the family needs feeding, so I cook and feed them. Daily kitchen jobs and chores are one thing, and the same old weekly menu pretty much reigns supreme in my kitchen from Monday to Friday. I have to adapt my repertoire to satisfy and feed a carnivorous husband who loves bread with most meals, a pescatarian daughter, two children addicted to pasta, and one who eats more than all six of us put together. Then there's me!

What do I like? Yes, of course pasta features very high on my daily food of choice, but it's what you add to your pasta and dress it with it that I want to focus on. During the week I need quick-to-cook recipes that pack a punch as well as covering most of our nutritional needs. When I'm working and writing from home, I take full advantage of my kitchen and biscuit barrel.

I will admit that I don't have the best of relationships with my slow cooker and prefer to slow-cook using my oven, unless I'm keeping my mulled wine warm – a winter essential. I just love dishes that have been cooked slowly. They never fail. Even the most novice of cooks can prepare a dish to slow-cook, like big meaty sauces made with pork ribs, where the meat falls off the bone, stirred through a thick robust pasta such as pappardelle, or spooned and served on top of freshly made Parmesan and cream polenta. Baked and layered dishes, risotto, gnocchi, slow-cooked casseroles with tender meat and seasonal vegetables can be made simple, too. The kind of casserole that you can add more to on a daily basis, referred to at Casa Carmela as 'The Bung In', is a family favourite.

So, back to that question, what or who inspires you?

I very rarely take inspiration from the celebrity chef world, though I do watch almost every cookery programme going – well, most of them – so that I remain 'on trend'. I love the passion and enthusiasm they show for real, unpretentious, honest food.

I choose not to write about faddy diets and ways of eating. I mean, how can people honestly cut all carbohydrates out of their diet? Just like a full-bodied wine, everything in moderation. Just eat a well-balanced Mediterranean diet and exercise regularly and you can't go far wrong.

I love to read cookery books from cover to cover – I take inspiration from the stories and tales before the recipe itself. I like to close my eyes and almost hear the chef's voice and passion for what they are writing about echo seamlessly over the pages, making me wish that I was a member of their family sitting at their kitchen table waiting patiently to be fed. The best cookbook is a thumbed, food-splattered and pencilled cookbook. How many of these do you own? I've lost count of mine.

My first cookery book, *Southern Italian Family Cooking*, is in essence my nonna (grandmother) Carmela and mother Solidea on a plate. It is a collection of our family recipes with my unique twist, built on love of the 'cucina povera' style of cooking. My second cookery book, *A Passion for Pasta*, is a beautifully photographed cookbook showcasing and depicting the regionality of delicious pasta dishes throughout the twenty incredibly varied regions of Italy. Writing *A Passion for Pasta*, I fell in love with each region and both of my cookery books inspired me to start this book you are now reading.

My inspiration for *Northern & Central Italian Family Cooking* comes not only from my first two cookbooks, but of course I have taken inspiration and guidance from the four very different seasons here in the UK, letting myself be influenced and gently led by what ingredients, such as seasonal fruit, vegetables, meat, game, shellfish, herbs and edible flowers, are available to us during each season. I hope my passion for Italian food from the northern and central regions spills over onto each page in the same way that I draw inspiration from my favourite Italian chefs as I read their books.

So, with that in mind, it's time to stock your store cupboard and fridge with essentials, turn on your favourite playlist and decide what to cook first.

Carmela's Italian store cupboard

Not much will come between me and my larder or pantry. I have what looks like a huge wardrobe in my kitchen. The difference being that when you open it, instead of my pretty dresses you'll find an array of essential ingredients that I like to keep in stock most of the time. As well as my larder wardrobe, I also have my much-loved and fully respected tomato cupboard which houses jars of passata, tomato concentrates and tins of tomatoes of all varieties, brands and styles. A well-stocked store cupboard will save you money, and if you have a little of everything you can muster up the most delicious healthy, fresh and seasonal meal at the drop of a hat.

ESSENTIAL INGREDIENTS
In order to produce simple, affordable, healthy dishes you will need to have a well-stocked larder, fridge and freezer. Here are my essential ingredients and staples to aid you in your cooking.

LARDER
Oils
- extra virgin olive oil, for finishing off dishes and salads (I use Filippo Berio)
- regular olive oil, for drizzling and light frying
- sunflower oil, for deep-frying

Vinegars
- An aged balsamic from Modena: I urge you not to buy one from the supermarket, but to search one out independently. I use the Giuseppe Giusti brand. I have visited the farm in Modena and adore the aroma and thickness that comes from every drop.
- red wine vinegar
- white wine vinegar

Tins and non-perishable ingredients
- A store cupboard full of tinned tomatoes and beans provide a basis to many dishes.
- passata (I use Mutti and Cirio brands)
- sun-dried tomatoes

- tinned beans: cannellini, chickpeas, butter beans, borlotti beans
- tinned fruit
- tinned tomatoes: plum
- tinned lentils
- tomato purée, to add flavour to soups, stocks and sauces

Jarred ingredients
- anchovy fillets, in brine, oil and salted: these subtly melt away while leaving a pleasant depth of saltiness to any dish.
- capers, in brine and salted: these berries add texture to dishes
- mostarda di frutta (Cremona): fruits steeped in a mustard syrup
- olives (a variety of green and black) with stones, in brine
- roasted red peppers

Dried herbs, spices and stock
Dried herbs and spices are essential store-cupboard ingredients. Just always remember that dried herbs have a more concentrated flavour than fresh and should be used sparingly. Also, ideally use them within their 'best before' date, before they lose their intensity.
- basil
- chilli flakes
- fennel seeds
- marjoram
- oregano
- pepper, black, freshly ground
- salt and rock salt (I use Maldon)
- stock cubes: chicken, vegetable, beef (good-quality)
- thyme
- vanilla: extract and whole pods

Flour
- '0' flour, for making bread, pasta and cakes
- '00' flour, an essential flour for making pasta, pizza and cakes
- self-raising flour: a staple flour for cake making
- semola/semolina flour (an Italian durum wheat flour): perfect for bread and pasta
- strong white bread flour: I use this combined with other flours to change the gluten levels and strength of doughs

Baking

- chocolate spread: I like Pan di Stelle
- dried fruit: sultanas, raisins
- ground almonds
- hard amaretto biscuits: I crush them and use them as a topping for tiramisu, cakes or ice cream
- jam (flavour of your choice)
- leaf gelatine
- mixed nuts: walnuts, hazelnuts, pistachios, pine nuts, almonds
- pane degli angeli: a traditional baking powder used in a range of Italian cakes and desserts

Dried pasta, sugar, pulses and grains

- stale/dried breadcrumbs
- lentils: red and green
- polenta: instant
- rice: arborio, carnaroli and vialone nano (I use the Riso Gallo brand)
- spaghetti, bucatini, ditalini, penne, trofie, rigatoni
- sugar: caster, granulated, golden

FRIDGE
Fresh herbs and spices

It is always preferable to use fresh herbs wherever possible, as they add a delicate flavour to any given dish. I use fresh herbs during each stage of cooking. Usually I add the chopped stems to a soffritto, then the leaves midway through cooking and also at the end as a garnish.

- basil
- bay
- fresh red chilli
- marjoram
- oregano
- rosemary
- sage
- thyme

Dairy

- butter: I use salted butter for all my needs
- lard: pork lard known in Italian as *strutto*

- cream: single and double
- eggs: all of the eggs used in this book are large and free-range
- milk: full-fat

Cheese
- buffalo mozzarella: torn into a salad – never cooked – as it is delicious simply dressed with a little extra virgin olive oil, salt and balsamic vinegar.
- dolcelatte: the sweeter and younger variety of gorgonzola
- fontina: a semi-hard cheese, creamy in texture and perfect for melting
- gorgonzola: mild and creamy cheese with a blue vein
- mascarpone: perfect for tiramisu, in desserts, stirred through roasted butternut squash and used to fill ravioli.
- mozzarella: made with cow's milk. Ideal to freeze and have in stock for using in layered pasta dishes and for topping pizza.
- Parmigiano-Reggiano: grate into pasta, risotto and more (never buy it pre-grated). Grated Parmigiano keeps incredibly well in the freezer.
- Pecorino Romano: sheep's cheese and an alternative to Parmigiano.
- provolone piccante: a Southern Italian cheese that is smooth in texture. Sliced thinly and eaten with bread, this is my father Rocco's and my favourite cheese.
- ricotta: ricotta does not melt ('ricotta' means 're-cooked'). Ideally, buy it from an Italian deli, or from a supermarket. I always choose the Galbani brand.
- Stracchino: a soft cheese, delicious scraped onto bread, spooned through pasta or served with a little honey.
- Taleggio: made with cow's milk and semi-soft. Very delicious.
- tomino: from Piedmont, ideal for baking (see page 69).

Cured meat
- bresaola: air-dried lean beef
- coppa: thinly sliced, dry-cured whole pork shoulder or neck
- guanciale: pig's cheek, delicious finely cubed in place of pancetta in a carbonara
- mortadella: re-formed pork, very delicious thinly sliced as part of an antipasti platter

- pancetta: from the pork belly area, thinly sliced or cubed
- prosciutto cotto: cooked ham
- prosciutto crudo: Parma ham
- salami: Milano, Napoli, ventricina, finocchiona
- speck: a cured and smoked ham, made from the hind leg of the pig, from the Trentino-Alto Adige region of Italy

Fresh vegetables
- vine tomatoes: cherry and plum, with the vines attached, kept at room temperature
- garlic: fresh bulbs
- shallots, celery and carrots: make the perfect soffritto, the base of many Italian sauces. You will notice that throughout this book I have chosen to use shallots instead of onions, as I find them easier to peel and prepare, and they're also a little sweeter.
- fennel bulb: an alternative to celery, and great in a soffritto.

FREEZER
- broad beans
- gelato
- mozzarella
- Parmigiano-Reggiano rinds
- mixed berries
- peas

LIQUOR
- amaretto
- Tia Maria
- Frangelico
- marsala
- white vermouth
- red vermouth

Alongside all of the above, you will just need to add leafy vegetables, root vegetables, fresh meat, fish and seafood.

CARMELA'S ESSENTIAL COOKERY TIPS
- Please do not discard Parmigiano rinds: they can be used in stocks, soups and risottos as flavour enhancers, particularly

when a dish is slow cooked. They also freeze well.
- Tomato vines can be added to soups, pasta water, sugo and standard sauces and stocks for added flavour. Once used, simply discard.
- When cooking fresh pasta, add a tablespoon of semola or '00' flour to the water once boiling point has been reached and prior to salting the water. The reason for this is because if fresh pasta only takes 3 or 4 minutes to cook, the water will have limited flavour, which is not what you want if you require the pasta water to emulsify your sauce. The flour releases gluten into the water, helping the pasta water thicken and emulsify your chosen sauce.
- Do not discard the milky liquid from a bag of fresh mozzarella. Added to flour to make pasta, bread, or pizza dough, it gives dough a delicate salty flavour and encompasses the *cucina povera* style of cooking. Alternatively, add it to stock, soups, or even your pasta cooking water.

EQUIPMENT
Pasta-making essentials
- chitarra: pasta guitar (this is not an essential but a worthwhile investment. The pasta alla chitarra can be cut by hand with a knife if you don't have this piece of kit)
- dough scraper
- fluted pastry wheel
- Marcato Atlas 150: a pasta machine
- pastry cutters: plain or fluted
- rolling pin or broom handle
- wooden board

COOK'S NOTES
How to sterilise jars
To sterilise your bottles or jars, wash them and put them in a low oven – about 140°C fan (325°F/gas 3) – until ready to fill, or put them in the dishwasher on a hot cycle with no detergent. Wash any rubber seals separately and dry them before filling and sealing the jars.

How to make breadcrumbs
Preheat the oven to 160°C fan (350°F/gas 4). Blitz stale bread in a

food processor until it forms crumbs, spread out on a baking tray and bake in the oven for 15 minutes. Remove from the oven and allow to cool, then return to the processor to blitz once again. Store in an airtight container for up to 3 months. I also use stale breadcrumbs, that are just blitzed in a food processor and not oven-dried, for ease and speed.

Leftover egg whites
Freeze leftover egg whites (for up to 6 months). They are a ideal for whipping up meringues or a seasonal frittata.

Seasonality

Seasonality brings with it not only an exceptional diversity of colour, aroma, flavour and richness but also a sense of excitement and hunger – a chance to try something that you long for from season to season, for example sweet British strawberries, delicate elderflowers, hedgerow berries, and the first bundle of asparagus you see in late spring. For the person that eats not only to survive but who savours each mouthful of food, then I am sure the change in seasons play a huge part in the way you learn to prepare, cook and enjoy your food too.

If you order a weekly vegetable box from a local greengrocer, a box of freshly caught fish-of-the-day from your fishmonger, or a selection of meat cuts from your butcher, each box is selected with the current season in mind. You will always have something different to try and, more importantly, it will give you the opportunity to try something that you many not necessarily choose, from wonky, dirty vegetables to an unattractive fish or cheap cuts of slightly fattier meat than you might usually go for.

Seasonal ingredients help you to stretch, alter and experiment with your weekly meal-plan, adding a little excitement and variety. I would always encourage you to take into consideration what's in season when you do your weekly food shop. For example, buying strawberries at Christmas to dress your trifle may not be the smartest decision, purely because you will be let down by their taste (even though they might look luscious and ruby-coloured). Buy them only in the summer when British strawberries reign supreme.

To remind me, and also to make my children aware of seasonal produce, I have a poster that I have stuck on the inside of my larder that tells me what to look out for month by month when I go food shopping, as well as what is growing in the garden and surrounding fields.

Foraging is not only a great way to grab some fresh air and help with mindfulness, but also, it's free – what you pick costs nothing. Take a basket and a pair of scissors out with you and only take what you need, don't pull up any plants, and please only forage if you know what you're looking for: mushrooms make a terrific find over the autumn months, but only a trained eye should pick them as there are many poisonous varieties around. Young spring nettles make a wonderful addition to pasta fillings and stews, and pan-fried foraged dandelion leaves add a bitter tang to many a side dish, or the flowers can be added to dress and perk up your salads.

In this book I will show you how to make the staple dishes of al dente pasta, silky risotto, full-of-flavour polenta and gorgeous gnocchi, while pairing them with the most amazing sauces and accompaniments. Get ready to fall in love with the taste and aromas of the four seasons.

A note on pasta, risotto, polenta and gnocchi

Pasta, risotto, polenta and gnocchi. They are delicious even when served nearly naked, with just a little browned butter, sage and salt, or with extra virgin olive oil, garlic and chilli, or a simple tomato sugo. They remain centre stage as I think they always should.

Pasta

In my opinion, fresh pasta really does surpass dried pasta hands down, and in an ideal world I would make it for my family more often than the current once-a-week Sunday stint I often do. Life tends to take over the rest of the week, so with no shame whatsoever, I stretch out my arm and open the fully stocked larder, aiming for my favourite shelf. Located at eye level, my dried pasta shelf houses at any one time between twenty-five and thirty bags of dried pasta (pasta secca). The pasta shapes have a diverse range of purposes, of course, and the brands I use are all-Italian, from De Cecco, La Molisana, Granoro and Pastificio G. Di Martino to La Fabbrica della Pasta di Gragnano, Rummo, Barilla and so many more.

With dried pasta the main rule is to always buy the best quality you can afford. Cheap dried pasta would make even the most delicious sauce taste unappealing.

My second cookbook features more than 100 Italian regional recipes, from the top of the mountains of Italy to the tip of the Italian boot. This book demonstrates how to pair seasonal produce with northern and central Italian flavours, while celebrating the British seasonality and showing you how to pair British produce with Italian ingredients and dishes, such as, pasta, risotto, polenta and gnocchi.

Rules for cooking pasta

1. Always use a large pan for cooking pasta.
2. Once boiling – and only when boiling – salt the water well. Pre-salting the water will slow down the rate at which your water will boil. As a guide, use 7–10g salt per litre of water and 100g pasta per litre of water. I'll leave you to do the maths for the amount you're cooking.
3. If you are cooking fresh pasta and will require a little of the pasta

water to aid in emulsifying your finished sauce, add a generous pinch of semola before salting the pasta water, to immediately begin the release of starchy gluten into the water.

Risotto

Hailing from the north of Italy, risotto is enjoyed with as much gusto throughout the country as traditional pasta. Risotto is a warming rice dish which offers a sense of autumnal comfort. However, in this book you will also find a favourite recipe of mine featuring a soft risotto made with prosecco and strawberries, perfect in the height of summer. Remember I said varied and diverse?

The main risotto rice grains accessible to us in the UK, and ones that I would recommend, are:

- Arborio: versatile and readily available, this is a great and widely used risotto rice.
- Carnaroli: a firm rice that holds its shape and is not easily overcooked.
- Vialone nano: a favourite rice of mine, however not so easy to come by. It is popular in the Veneto region of Italy and has an intense creaminess.

Risotto should be made when you have a little time on your hands. It's the ideal opportunity to stir uninterrupted with, in an ideal world, a glass of wine and a little background jazz.

The risotto should be the queen of the dish, however the flavourings paired with it are also key. Spring risotto echoes flavours of spring pea and lemon, while summer beckons pan-fried courgette with a filled courgette flower nestled very daintily on top. Autumn, my favourite season, calls for a wild foraged mushroom risotto, and winter finishes with a wild boar or rabbit ragù risotto, or even a rich, deep, decadent Barbaresco risotto with crumbled gorgonzola.

Seasonal ingredients, a well-seasoned stock and a wooden spoon (preferably one with a hole in the centre) is all you need. Stir well, throughout cooking, to encourage the creaminess of the starch to come out of the grains, and remember to allow the risotto to rest before serving: cover the pan with a clean tea towel then a lid and leave for 5-10 minutes before serving. This stage is called 'la mantecatura' and it is very important: it allows the risotto to rest and ooze creaminess once the finishing fat has been added and the pan removed from the heat. I have also included a few baked risotto dishes for an easy, no-stir alternative.

Polenta

When I think of polenta I immediately smile and go back to my roots of peasant-style cooking, known as 'cucina povera'. From humble beginnings come delicious things. Polenta is a grain that is not only naturally gluten-free, but also incredibly versatile. For speed, you can use quick-cook polenta (available in most supermarkets), which takes between five and ten minutes to cook. Polenta bramata takes a little longer to cook, close to an hour in fact, so ensure you have time and energy to stand and stir it until it's ready. Pre-cooked polenta is also available in supermarkets, sold in blocks for budget cooking, though I really would recommend you steer clear of these.

Polenta is known as cornmeal, and as grits in the USA. Polenta bramata (the long-cook variety) is a coarse yellow grain.

There are two variations of the dish: wet and firm. For wet polenta, the polenta is stirred with water, stock or milk and finished with a knob of butter and grated Parmigiano, or served with soft stracchino cheese – scrumptious to say the least. Wet polenta makes a perfect base for pan-fried mushrooms and thyme, slow-cooked venison ragù or delicious seafood with cherry tomatoes. To make firmer-textured polenta, the cooked polenta is spooned into a lined tray and left to cool then chill in the fridge, then after an hour or so it is sliced, pan-fried and topped with toppings of your choice. When I visited Venice in the region of Veneto I enjoyed polenta slices with delicious toppings, my favourite being baccalà (creamy salt cod). The polenta cicchetti in Venice is often made with white polenta.

Polenta can also be used to coat fish, chicken and potatoes, to add texture and crunch.

Gnocchi

These small dough pillows, from potato gnocchi to beautiful light gnudi and malfatti, all but melt in the mouth. Made with potatoes, ricotta, eggs, flour, semola, herbs and vegetables, all in various combinations, gnocchi also varies in size. Once the dough has been made it is portioned and rolled into long sausages, then cut into small pieces and either rolled down the prongs of a fork or shaped using a wooden gnocchi board.

Cook gnocchi in a saucepan of salted water. You will know when it's ready as the cooked gnocchi will float to the top of the pan. Leave for a further two or three minutes then remove gently with a slotted spoon, add sauce and serve immediately with grated Parmigiano or Pecorino. Pre-made fresh potato gnocchi are also available in vacuum-packed bags in the fridge aisle, and dried gnocchi can be found in your supermarket's dried pasta aisle. Gnudi or malfatti are made with ricotta, spinach, egg, nutmeg and a scant amount of flour instead of potatoes. Formed into small balls the size of walnuts, or perfectly formed quenelles, they can be boiled gently for a couple of minutes, drained and dressed in sage and browned butter or a little drizzle of pesto. Delicious indeed. Serving gnocchi with seasonal vegetables, slow-cooked venison ragù, or a simple drizzle of extra virgin olive oil showcases not only seasonality but how fantastic a simple Italian dumpling can be.

Aperitivo e Digestivo

Aperitivo time has to be the best part of the day, especially if you're in the north of Italy, mainly Milan. Aperitivo means 'the opener', the beginning of your forthcoming meal. Between 7pm and 9pm, after you've finished work, you pop along to a bar for a refreshing cocktail or drink to prepare you and arouse your hunger. It is a social gathering for a pre-meal drink and light bites.

The drinks tend to be slightly bitter, and they pair perfectly with salty snack offerings. Snacks and small bites are offered with both alcoholic and non-alcoholic beverages during the aperitivo hours. An Italian lunch tends to be eaten between 1pm and 2pm most days, so your evening meal is usually eaten later at night.

Here are a few of my favourite aperitivi suggestions for you to try: Begin with a bitter ruby Campari with a slice of orange, or a slightly sweeter, more feminine, Aperol spritz finished with a spritz of orange peel, orange slice and an optional olive garnish, a simple yet classic Martini (rosso or bianco), or the godfather of the cocktail world in my opinion – the negroni. A negroni is a combination of gin, Campari and red vermouth, but I have to say I do love the sweeter sister 'negroni sbagliato', which replaces the gin with prosecco.

To finish your meal, I would suggest you order a digestivo. You could try an Amaro digestivo, a short dark drink made with a blend of spices. It's a rich after-dinner, velvety, bittersweet drink, and it has endless options and possibilities (whether you serve it with or without ice is at your discretion). A few others I'd recommend are: Averna, Cynar, Montenegro, Ramazzotti, Fernet Branca and the wonderful Amaro Lucano.

From a perfectly poured and mixed welcome drink, to a homemade bottle of liquor that you can gift with a beautifully tied ribbon, aperitivi and digestivi can define your meal, evening or dinner party.

Non-alcoholic Aperitivi

A non-alcoholic aperitivi would be the perfect start to a long, lazy lunch. Non-alcoholic beverages are increasingly popular, and rightly so. Many diners choose not to drink alcohol, so why should they miss out? They shouldn't, and I am happy to say that in Italy, as well as in the UK, they don't. Most bars, restaurants and cafés in Italy offer a selection of bitters, as well as their own take on regional cocktails that are made with beautiful fruits and sodas rather than alcohol.

A wonderful amber bitter that I frequently offer at my supper club is Crodino, a bitter non-alcoholic orange drink, served over ice with a slice of twisted orange. It's simple and refreshing. You can also find a slightly fruitier version of Crodino called a Crodino Twist. Try to search out these alternative options and purchase a few to have in stock at home.

A few other popular finds to serve over ice:

- San Pellegrino Sanbitter and Sanbitter Bianco
- Chinotto: a myrtle-leaf orange drink. Chinotto is a bitter drink, the same colour of coke but with no sweetness.
- Tassoni Cedrata: a sparkling, almost citrussy, drink and a firm favourite flavour of mine. Serve over ice with a slice of lemon or lime.
- Spuma Nera: referred to as the 'mother' of Chinotto, with the addition of rhubarb, orange zest and vanilla.
- Gingerino: an orange drink with a twist of warmth from ginger.
- San Pellegrino non-alcoholic cocktail drinks: serve over ice with a twist of fresh orange.
- Monte Rosso: a non-alcoholic drink similar to Campari, made with rowanberries and cranberries. Serve over ice with a slice of orange.

Amaretto Sour

I adore an amaretto on the rocks, its natural amber warmth poured over ice cubes and offered up in an old-fashioned thick-glassed tumbler. Timeless and moreish with every sip. An amaretto sour simply adds to the liqueur a sour kick from freshly juiced lemons and a sense of opulence from the egg white. Maraschino cherries in syrup are a necessity here, for their pure deep colour and delicious texture. Simplicity is key.

Makes: 4
You will need: 2 old-fashioned tumbler glasses and a cocktail shaker

ice cubes
60ml Disaronno amaretto liqueur
30ml freshly squeezed lemon juice
about 15g egg white
2–4 maraschino cherries (I use Luxardo)

1. Fill the two glasses with ice cubes.
2. Put the amaretto liqueur, lemon juice and egg white in a cocktail shaker, clamp on the lid and shake vigorously to emulsify (don't add ice before you shake).
3. Strain into the ice-filled glasses and add a maraschino cherry or two.

CARMELA'S TIP:
- It is vital here to use fresh, free-range eggs. 15g is the typical weight of an egg white from 1 large, free-range egg.

Amber Spritz, *Spritz Veneziano*

A bitter cocktail that, dare I say, you either love or don't. I adore the bitter fragrant notes with the added sliced orange and optional olive. As I sip, I feel like I could almost be that Venetian princess I long to be, sitting, people-watching and smiling at the beauty that is the busy and somewhat hectic Venetian canal. Could I truly visit Venice (Veneto) and not have enjoyed a few spritzes? Of course not.

Makes: 3
You will need: 3 wine glasses

ice cubes
100ml Aperol
150ml dry prosecco
sparkling water, for topping up
2 orange slices
green olive (optional)

I am not too methodical when it comes to the preparation of a spritz, as it's easy enough (hence no measurements above).

1. Fill the glasses with ice at least three-quarters of the way up.
2. Divide the Aperol between the 3 glasses.
3. Divide the prosecco between the 3 glasses and top up with sparkling water.
4. Garnish with a slice of orange (and I love to add an olive).

CARMELA'S TIP:
- If you find Aperol a little bitter, reduce the amount of Aperol and increase the prosecco. Or, try a Cynar spritz by mixing 50ml Cynar with 50ml prosecco and 50ml sparkling water, and garnishing with orange, berries and mint to serve.

Cinico, from Venice with love

Everyone who enjoys aperitivo while visiting Venice can generally be found either sipping overpriced peach bellinis in Harry's Bar or sitting and people-watching with large amber-filled glasses of freshly made spritz, a slice of orange and an olive in St Mark's Square. I adore drinking both, for obvious reasons, but on my most recent trip to the beautiful city my friend Monica introduced me to Cinico, an Italian cinnamon liquor which was offered to me in a tall glass with a mint leaf and cinnamon stick. All I will say is you must try one, or possibly two, when you're next in Venice – or try making one.

Makes: 2
You will need: 2 large wine glasses

ice cubes
6 mint leaves, slightly bruised
2 lime wedges
100ml Cinico (cinnamon liqueur)
150ml prosecco
sparking water, for topping up
2 cinnamon sticks, garnish

1. Fill the large glasses with ice cubes.
2. Add 3 bruised mint leaves to each glass, along with a wedge of lime.
3. Pour 50ml of the cinnamon liqueur into each glass. Add the prosecco and top up with sparkling water.
4. Add a cinnamon stick to each glass for a final garnish and touch of spice.

Espresso Martini

Now we enter the territory of ultimate perfection. Fresh coffee, sugar syrup and coffee liqueur. Sophistication of the highest kind, dressed with a solitary coffee bean. The ingredients and preparation here are key, and never forget to use a long-stemmed glass with a wide mouth.

Makes: 2
You will need: 2 chilled martini glasses and a cocktail shaker

100g golden caster sugar
50ml water
ice cubes
100ml vodka (I use Black Cow)
50ml cooled espresso coffee
50ml coffee liqueur (I use Borghetti)
coffee beans (optional)

1. Make a sugar syrup by heating the caster sugar in a small saucepan with the 50ml of water over a medium heat. Bring to the boil and cook for 3 minutes until the sugar has dissolved, then remove from the heat and allow the syrup to fully cool.
2. Put 1 tablespoon of the cooled syrup in a cocktail shaker. Fill with ice cubes and add the vodka, cooled espresso coffee and liqueur. Clamp on the lid and shake really well.
3. Pour the liquid through a strainer into your martini glasses and garnish with coffee beans if you wish.

CARMELA'S TIPS:
- The remaining sugar syrup will keep in the fridge for up to 7 days.
- If you are unable to source Borghetti, Tia Maria or Kahlua will work just as well.

Fennel Gin and Tonic

'A refreshing gin and tonic, please.' You can hear these are words echoing on repeat in most UK bars. The increasing number of flavoured gins and distilleries popping up in this country is incredible. This is a wonderful thing because the range of flavours available are so diverse; some are delicious and some not so much. I like to use Malfy gins – they are fresh and offer the kinds of flavours which complement my mood. However, a beautiful, simple unflavoured gin is also just divine. In my favourite fennel and gin cocktail I have chosen to opt for the original Malfy gin so that the notes of the fennel can shine through. I love the intense aroma and flavour of aniseed; I'm sure it will become a favourite of yours, too.

Makes: Use the proportions below to make as many as you like
You will need: a chilled glass

ice cubes
1-part gin
2-parts tonic water
sliced fresh fennel (fronds optional)

1. Take a chilled gin glass and add 3 cubes of ice.
2. Pour in the gin and add the tonic.
3. Add sliced fennel as required, and the fronds too (if you like).

CARMELA'S TIP:
- As I mentioned, I do like Malfy gin, however a great alternative would be Gin Mare, widely available in many UK supermarkets.

Homemade Fig-leaf Gin

This is a gin that I typically make at the end of our fig season in the UK, which is in late summer or early autumn. My fig tree usually fails to provide me with bountiful fruit, but it does gift me with giant, fragrant leaves instead. This I don't really mind, as I have fruit from my nonna Carmela's tree, and also my uncle Leonardo's incredible plump green figs to rely on. So, I am now looking radiantly plump and full of figs and can make my favourite liqueur with the leaves. Make the liqueur as soon as you are in possession of the fig leaves as it will require 3 months waiting time until it's ready.

Makes: one 750ml bottle
Preparation time: 15 minutes
Cooking time: 20 minutes
Resting time: at least 3 months
You will need: 1 sterilised 750ml bottle (see page 9 for sterilising instructions)

300g caster sugar
370ml water
8 fresh fig leaves
360ml gin (a plain, original gin)

1. Put the sugar and water in a small saucepan over a medium heat and allow the sugar to dissolve, then add the fig leaves.
2. Cook the syrup with the fig leaves over a medium-low heat for 15 minutes, then remove from the heat and allow the leaves to cool in the syrup.
3. Once cool, squeeze and wring out the fig leaves over the pan of syrup then discard the fig leaves.
4. Pour the syrup into the sterilised bottle and top with your chosen gin. Seal and forget about the gin, placing it at the back of a cupboard for at least 3 months. The longer the better as this will intensify the flavour.
5. Serve the gin neat, over ice, or with a little tonic of your choice.

CARMELA'S TIPS:
- If there is a gap in the top of the bottle, top it up with cooled, boiled water.
- The fig leaf syrup can also be added to a little soda water, stirred and topped with a mint leaf to make a non-alcoholic drink.

Italicus Rosolio di Bergamotto

Sophisticated and timeless, Italicus is more than just the stylish bottle. It has to be one of my favourite drinks. This is hardly a recipe, I know, but it's a drink nonetheless that I would recommend you try. Italicus is made using a blend of botanicals from floral notes of rose and lavender to finishing citrus flavours. It's so classic served over ice with an olive or two.

Makes: Use the proportions below to make as many as you like
You will need: a chilled martini glass

crushed ice
1-part Italicus
1-part prosecco
1–2 olives per glass (Nocellara are my favourite)

1. Add a little crushed ice to a martini glass.
2. Add one-part Italicus to one-part prosecco.
3. Stir and tumble in an olive or two.
4. Enjoy.

Peach Bellini

When made well, and in the summer season, a peach bellini is simply stunning, from the colour to the balanced sweetness. But, seeing as I love a peach bellini the whole year round, I will give you a few options. Out of the summer season it's best to use peach purée instead of juice, if you are able to find it, but I use tinned peaches. Can I be honest for a moment? I love tinned fruit as a quick pudding and I always have them available, even if they're right at the back of my larder. They work as a great emergency option – there's no need for any embarrassment or food snobbery.

Makes: 4 peach bellinis
You will need: 4 chilled champagne flutes

6 ripe, flat white peaches
(or a 200g tin of peaches if making a tinned fruit bellini)
750ml prosecco

I will give you three methods, simply choose your preferred one.

Roasted Peach Bellini

Cooking time: 20 minutes

1. Preheat the oven to 180°C fan (400°F/gas 6).
2. Halve the peaches and remove the stones.
3. Place the peach halves on a baking tray and bake in the oven for 20 minutes until they are softened and slightly browning on the edges. Larger peaches may take a little longer.
4. Remove from the oven, peel off and discard the peach skins and blitz the roasted peach halves in a blender or food processor, then pass through a sieve. Spoon the fruit purée into chilled champagne flutes.
5. Top with prosecco, stir and devour.

Sliced Peach Bellini

1. Slice the peaches, removing the stones.
2. Place the fruit in a blender and pulse into a purée.
3. Pass through a sieve to remove fibrous pieces and fragments. Taste and add a little sugar syrup (see page 22) if needed.
4. Spoon into chilled champagne flutes.
5. Top with prosecco, enjoy.

Tinned Fruit Bellini

1. Put 200g tinned peaches, including the juice, in a blender or food processor and blitz.
2. Pass through a sieve and spoon the fruit purée into chilled champagne flutes.
3. Top with prosecco.

Raspberrycello, *Liquore di lamponi*

An alternative use for the ruby pink, plump raspberries of late summer is my take on a simple yet vibrant liqueur. It's light yet fruity and, dare I say it, when added to a long glass with a little ice and prosecco, it's almost virginal. I make as many bottles as possible and give them away as gifts, however the bottle that I have opened lives happily in my freezer, ensuring it's ready for an impromptu drink. It's delicious just with ice, or added to prosecco.

Makes: 750ml
Resting time: 3 weeks
You will need: 1 x 1.5 litre sterilised jar plus 2 x 375ml sterilised bottles (see page 9 for sterilising instructions)

250g raspberries, washed and dried
250g granulated sugar
750ml vodka

1. Add the raspberries and sugar to the sterilised jar. Pour in the vodka, stir and seal.
2. Shake the jar daily to allow the raspberries to permeate the vodka, creating a stunning vibrant pink colour.
3. After about 3 weeks, when the alcohol is ready, strain the raspberrycello through a piece of clean muslin to remove the berries and any sediment or residue.
4. Pour the strained liquid into your 2 sterilised bottles and freeze until required. Make sure you leave at least a couple of centimetres gap at the top of the bottle so the glass doesn't crack in the freezer.

CARMELA'S TIPS:
- You can replace the vodka with gin.
- This liqueur will keep for up to a year in the freezer (it can be kept at room temperature too, but it tastes better from the freezer). Keep one bottle and gift the second.

Sorbet served with Vodka and Prosecco,
Sgroppino

Refreshing, light and perfect as a treat on a long, hot summer's day. 'Is sgroppino a dessert?', I hear you ask. I would class it as an either/or. It can be a drink or a light, after-dinner palate cleanser, but I would opt for the first. For speed, I tend to use a good-quality shop-bought lemon sorbet, however the flavour is entirely up to you.

Serves: 2
You will need: 2 chilled, long-stemmed martini glasses

> 2 small scoops of lemon sorbet (or watermelon sorbet)
> 30ml vodka (I use Black Cow)
> prosecco, for topping up
> 2 basil leaves, to garnish

1. Put a scoop of your chosen sorbet into each chilled glass.
2. Add 15ml of vodka to each glass and top up as required with prosecco.
3. Garnish with a basil leaf.

CARMELA'S TIP:
- For a child-friendly version, add a little fresh fruit juice to the sorbet with a mint leaf, instead of the alcohol.

The Negroni, *La Rossa*

The negroni is a much-loved cult cocktail, a favourite in bars not only in Italy but across the world. Fiery in colour, with a distinct aromatic taint of bitter richness, it has always held its own – a classic with a sophisticated twist. Make mine a large one, please! The purists among us stick to the rules and this recipe does just that, requiring no alterations, tweaks or improvements. You simply cannot improve on perfection.

Makes: Use the proportions below to make as many as you like
You will need: a chilled glass

ice cubes
1-part gin
1-part sweet vermouth
1-part Campari
1 slice of orange

1. Add 4 or 5 ice cubes to a chilled glass.
2. Add one-part gin, 1-part vermouth and 1-part Campari to a mixing glass with 2 ice cubes and stir.
3. Strain into your prepared glass and garnish with a slice of orange.

CARMELA'S TIP:
- I love my negroni to be served over ice in a small, wide glass tumbler, however a martini glass will elevate the sophistication and, as for many cocktails, the ice cubes are optional.

Tomato Vine Liqueur, *Liquore al pomodoro*

The humble tomato fruit is a joy on its own merit and I would be lost without these rosy, voluptuous beauties adorning my kitchen windowsill. When ripe, they have a wonderful, juicy sweetness and pair perfectly with almost everything. Tomatoes are the epitome of Italian cooking. The vines are what house the intense aroma that we all love when we think of tomatoes. I have used the vines in my cooking for years, adding them to my slow-cooked meat sugos, stocks and soups. Once used, I discard them. They are a fantastic flavour enhancer, so be sure to use them when you can. Here, I steep the vines in neat vodka to obtain a fragrant tomato aroma and lovely delicate back-note. This would make a wonderful addition to a Bloody Mary with a sprig of celery.

Makes: 700ml
Preparation time: 5 minutes
Steeping time: 1 month minimum
You will need: 1 x 750ml sterilised Kilner-style jar (see page 9 for sterilising instructions)

700ml vodka
10–12 fragrant tomato vines

1. Pour the vodka into a sterilised jar.
2. Take the tomato vines and crush them in your hands to wake up the aroma.
3. Place the vines in the vodka and close the lid firmly.
4. Shake the jar and leave the tomato vines to steep in the vodka for at least a month.
5. After a month, strain and rebottle.

Spring

The first hope of spring, the first bulb that pops through the ground, leads us gently by the hand as we skip into warmer, brighter days. The clocks spring forward, the days grow longer and the new season introduces us to a welcome change of ingredients.

The shift in my seasonal cooking is showcased by this change of vegetables, fruits and herbs. Spring gives us beautiful fluffy Parma Violet-coloured chive flowers, with their delicate leaves and unique oniony sweetness; it gives us dandelions, a weed with a bitter savoury note that is delicious and, contrary to what we were told as children if we picked these sunshine-looking flowers, does not make us wet the bed. Forage for them in the spring as this is when they are at their most tender, using the heads in salads and frittatas and the leaves pan-fried as a side. Delicate herbs may be growing in your garden, too, and let's not forget about the wild garlic season.

My style of cooking changes, with dishes becoming a little lighter, and I introduce floral notes, though my food still has a resounding warmth to it.

This chapter gives you soups a plenty, with my favourite being stracciatella, a dish of whipped egg in stock and barley soup. You will also find fresh Ligurian pesto, spaghetti frittata, cuttlefish ink risotto, baccalà and baked tomino cheese from Piedmont, to name just a few.

Barley Soup, *Zuppa d'orzo*

Any warm soup offers a sense of comfort, however a barley soup also has the ability to hold its texture at the same time. This dish is full of fibre and is willing to take on whatever you choose to throw at it. I prefer to cook barley in the form of a soup rather than in the style of a risotto, because it doesn't have the natural ability to ooze creaminess. So, barley, know your place!

Serves: 4
Preparation time: 15 minutes
Cooking time: 1 hour 20 minutes

180g barley, rinsed
1.5 litres hot vegetable stock
1 small leek, washed well and finely chopped
1 medium carrot, peeled and finely cubed
1 celery stick, finely cubed
1 large or 2 medium potatoes, peeled and finely cubed
2 tbsp finely chopped celery leaves
150g smoked pancetta, finely chopped
salt and freshly ground black pepper

To serve
2 tbsp chopped chives
rustic bread

1. Put the barley in a 3-litre saucepan with the hot stock and cook over a medium heat for 25 minutes.
2. After 25 minutes add the leek, carrot, celery, potatoes and half the celery leaves, then season with salt and pepper and cook for a further 30 minutes.
3. In the meantime, fry the pancetta in a small dry frying pan over a medium heat for 10 minutes, until lightly coloured all over.
4. Add the pancetta and residual fat from the pan to the soup and stir. Taste and check once again for additional seasoning and add the remaining celery leaves.
5. Ladle the soup into warm bowls, sprinkle over the chopped chives and serve with rustic bread.

CARMELA'S TIP:
- For a vegetarian version, simply leave out the pancetta.

Chicken Soup with Toasted Bread and Egg, *Zuppa pavese*

Medicinal comfort in a bowl. If you're unable to make or source fresh chicken stock, then don't make this dish as the stock is key. Without a flavourful fresh stock, the dish simply wouldn't work, so allow time by prepping and making the stock in advance. The key to a traditional zuppa pavese is an excruciatingly hot soup bowl, toasted bread, raw egg and hot stock to naturally cook the egg. The brave will opt for the traditional method of pavese, however feel free to pop the finished dish in the oven for 5 minutes to cook the egg a little more, if you prefer.

Serves: 4 as a breakfast, starter or lunch
Preparation time: 15 minutes
Cooking time: 1 hour 30 minutes

60g salted butter
2 tbsp olive oil
4 slices of rustic bread
4 eggs
40g Parmigiano-Reggiano, grated
salt and freshly ground black pepper

For the chicken stock
2 free-range chicken legs
2 free-range chicken thighs
1 celery stick, roughly chopped
2 plum tomatoes, quartered
1 shallot, halved, with the peel left on
1 carrot, peeled and roughly chopped
small bunch of celery leaves, roughly chopped
small bunch of parsley, roughly chopped
tomato vine (optional)

1. Put the chicken thighs and legs in a large saucepan and fill the pan with water. Bring to a steady boil and add the celery, quartered tomatoes, shallot (including the peel), carrot, celery and parsley leaves and the tomato vine (if using).

2. Season with salt and pepper, bring the liquid to a steady simmer and cook over a medium heat for about 1 hour 30 minutes, skimming off and discarding any scum that appears on the surface with a spoon. Taste and check for additional seasoning intermittently throughout cooking.

3. Remove the chicken and place to one side to serve later in the meal, or at another meal.

4. Strain the stock through a sieve into a clean pan and use a potato masher to squash the vegetables through the sieve. Use a clean spatula to scrape the vegetable goodness from the base of the sieve into the pan.

5. Discard the thick residue from the inside of the sieve as this is no longer required. Taste and season the stock and keep it bubbling gently over a medium heat.

6. Heat the oven to 150°C fan (325°F/gas 3) and place four soup bowls in the oven to warm.

7. Melt the butter in a frying pan over a medium heat and add the oil, add the bread and fry until lightly toasted and golden on both sides.

8. Place a slice of toasted bread into each hot bowl.

9. Crack an egg carefully onto each slice of bread. Sprinkle a little salt onto each yolk and top with a sprinkle of Parmigiano.

10. Pour a ladle of hot stock over the egg and serve immediately. The stock should partially cook the white of the egg. The yolk should burst and be stirred directly into the stock.

CARMELA'S TIPS:
- For a firmer egg, finish cooking the egg in the oven for a few minutes once it's added to the toast.
- Prepare and make the stock up to 3 days in advance, to save time.

Chickpea Pancake, *Farinata di ceci*

Farinata di ceci (or *cecina*) is known by many names and is well recognised outside Italy, although Liguria seems to have a firm grip on it as its chosen regional dish. It is, in essence, an un-leavened pancake, made even better. I simply adore the taste of farinata as it has such a satisfying texture – it is almost eggy, yet it has a firm bite, and it is equally delicious hot or cold. The simplicity of this snack alone will ensure it becomes a family favourite at your kitchen table. A mix of chickpea flour, water, salt and oil has never tasted so good.

Serves: 4–6
Preparation time: 5 minutes, plus 2–4 hours resting time
Cooking time: 24 minutes
You will need: a foil or regular baking tray about 27 x 37cm and 2.5cm deep

900ml cold water
300g chickpea flour
10g salt (I use Maldon sea salt)
40ml extra virgin olive oil

1. Pour the water into a large bowl. Slowly incorporate the chickpea flour, whisking constantly, until the mixture is smooth. Add the salt and stir.
2. Cover the bowl and allow it to rest in the fridge for as long as possible. I would recommend a minimum of 2 hours chilling at least (and up to 4 hours).
3. Preheat the oven to 240°C fan (500°F/gas 9) and line the baking tray with baking parchment. Clear the base of the oven as that's where you'll need to place your tray initially.
4. Take the farinata mix out of the fridge. With a large spoon, gently scoop off the foam (*scuma*) and discard.
5. Whisk again to awaken the mix and pour in the extra virgin olive oil. Whisk to incorporate.
6. Take your pre-lined tray and pour in the farinata mix, creating a thin layer. Bake it in the base of the oven for 10 minutes.

7. After 10 minutes, reduce the oven temperature to 220°C fan (475°F/gas 8) and place the tray in the middle of the oven for a further 14 minutes, until the farinata is lightly golden and set to the touch.
8. Remove the farinata from the oven and allow to cool a little, then remove the parchment, slice and enjoy.
9. Serve hot or cold, as a snack, in a panino or as part of your antipasti feast.

CARMELA'S TIP:
- Add a sprinkle of fresh sliced chilli to the batter for a little heat.

Creamy salt cod, *Baccalà mantecato*

Veneto at its best! This recipe is from my good friend Monica Cesarato and her business partner Arianna who together run the 'Cook in Venice' cookery school. I have known Monica for years and when making the *baccalà mantecato*, her passion, knowledge and expertise most certainly shone through. She says, 'Whisk, whisk, and when you think it's ready, whisk some more.' If you choose to whisk by hand, in all honestly you may struggle depending on the quantity you choose to make. A stand mixer fitted with a whisk attachment makes the entire experience a worthwhile and, dare I say it, pleasurable one.

Serves: 6, alongside antipasti
Preparation time: 30 minutes, plus 2 days' soaking
Cooking time: 20 minutes

1kg baccalà or stockfish
400ml full-fat milk
400ml water
1 garlic clove, peeled but left whole
about 250ml sunflower oil
about 15g salt (I suggest you constantly taste to adjust the seasoning)
4 tbsp extra virgin olive oil
2 tbsp finely chopped parsley
crostini or firm polenta cut into cicchetti-sized squares, as required (NB: cicchetti means small Italian dishes similar to tapas style)

1. Two days before serving, place the baccalà or stockfish in a large bowl of cold water. Leave it to soak in the fridge for 2 days, discarding and replenishing the water every few hours to remove the salt and rehydrate the fish.
2. After two days' soaking, drain the rehydrated fish, cut it into smaller pieces and put the pieces in a large saucepan. Cover the fish with the milk and water. Bring to a simmer over a medium heat and clamp on a lid. Simmer for 15 minutes.
3. Remove from the heat and allow the fish to cool in the liquid.

4. When cool enough to handle, remove the fish from the milky water, saving the liquid for later. Remove the skin from the fish, reserving half of it. Pick the flesh away from the bones – make sure you are incredibly thorough – and place into a clean bowl. Cut the reserved skin into thin strips and add it to the bowl.

5. Place the fish in a stand mixer fitted with a whisk attachment and add the garlic clove, 200ml of the reserved milky cooking liquid and 100ml of the sunflower oil.

6. Whisk the mixture for about 15 minutes, starting at low speed and slowly increasing the speed as you whisk, then continue to add the remaining sunflower oil in a slow and steady stream as you would if you were making a classic mayonnaise, until the baccalà looks creamy and delicately soft. You may not need to use all of the oil, so pour with caution. Taste and check for seasoning, adding salt as required.

7. Remove the garlic clove, then add the extra virgin olive oil and stir.

8. Serve on crostini or polenta squares with a sprinkle of fresh parsley.

CARMELA'S TIP:
- Baccalà and stockfish are both preserved and air-dried cod, but baccalà is also salted.

Cuttlefish Ink Risotto, *Risotto al nero di seppia*

This creamy risotto has an intensity from the ocean. The best risotto nero I've ever tasted was from one of my wonderful research trips to Venice (Veneto). It was deep in colour, balanced, and had echoes of a mildly creaminess that is somewhat tricky to recreate without the help of butter and a ludicrous amount of Parmigiano. The cuttlefish ink and gentle stirring action seems to give the perfect balance of softness, but please feel free to finish the risotto with a little butter if the desire takes you.

Serves: 6
Preparation time: 15 minutes
Cooking time: 40 minutes, plus resting time

1.2 litres fresh fish stock
4 tbsp olive oil
1 large shallot, finely chopped
1 celery stick, finely chopped
2 garlic cloves, crushed
small bunch of parsley, chopped (including stems)
650g cuttlefish, cleaned and thinly sliced, plus any tentacles
1 small fresh red chilli, deseeded and finely chopped
4 fresh plum tomatoes, quartered
500g vialone nano or carnaroli risotto rice
125ml dry white wine
2 x 7g sachets of cuttlefish ink
1 tbsp finely chopped celery leaves
60g salted butter
salt

1. Place a 2-litre saucepan on the hob, add the fish stock and warm it gently over a medium heat. Taste and ensure that the stock is not overly salty. If it is, dilute it with a little water.
2. Heat the olive oil in a separate large saucepan over a medium heat, add the shallot and celery and cook over a medium heat for about 10 minutes until softened. Add the garlic and parsley stems and stir.

3. Tumble in the prepared cuttlefish, chilli and tomatoes, stir and cook for 5 minutes.

4. Add your chosen risotto rice and toast it, stirring, for 1 minute, then pour in the wine. Stir until the wine has been absorbed.

5. Squeeze the ink sachets into the risotto and stir until every grain has begun to turn a deep shade of black.

6. Slowly begin to add the fish stock, one ladle at a time, stirring frequently with a wooden spoon that has a hole in the centre (if you have one) for about 20 minutes until the rice has absorbed the stock. Taste and season as you go. Almost 5 minutes before the risotto is ready, when the risotto becomes al dente, add the celery leaves and stir. Once cooked, check for additional seasoning.

7. Remove from the heat and add the parsley leaves and butter. Stir, cover the pan with a clean tea towel and clamp on a lid. Let the risotto rest, covered for 5–10 minutes before serving.

CARMELA'S TIP:

- You can easily substitute cuttlefish for squid, as it tends to be much easier to come by in its freshest form and offers an instant sweetness. Also, I sometimes make this risotto with water or vegetable stock and not with fish stock – my mood dictates which stock I use.

Dandelions with Garlic, Chilli and Olives,

Cicoria con aglio, peperoncino e olive

Bittersweet foraged dandelion makes this dish a perfect late-spring treasure. I use the sunshine head of the dandelion in salads and pan-fry the stalks and leaves. Dandelions are best picked during the spring months as they have a slightly sweeter taste, but often they still hold their notorious bitter flavour, too. They work perfectly as a side dish to a piece of fish or meat, tossed through pasta or – my favourite – squashed in between a panino filled with a little cured meat, a spicy provolone cheese and the warm pan-fried dandelion greens.

Serves: 4
Preparation time: 5 minutes
Cooking time: 8–10 minutes

400g freshly foraged dandelions
3–4 tbsp extra virgin olive oil
1 shallot, thinly sliced
1 plump garlic clove, thinly sliced
40g pitted green olives, sliced
small fresh chilli(es), thinly sliced (quantity is your choice)
salt and freshly ground black pepper
basil leaves, torn, to serve

1. Wash the dandelions well in a little salted water.
2. Remove the heads of the dandelions and set them aside on some kitchen paper. Place them in the fridge and use the heads within 12 hours in a seasonal salad or as a garnish.
3. Separate the stems and the leaves and roughly chop the stems.
4. Add the stems and leaves to a saucepan of salted boiling water and cook for 5 minutes. Drain the greens well and set them aside.
5. Heat the oil in a shallow frying pan over a low heat and add the sliced shallot and garlic. Fry gently for 4 minutes or so, until the shallot has just softened, then tumble in the olives and add the drained greens. Stir well and cook for a further 2 minutes. Add the sliced chilli and season well with salt and pepper.

6. Remove from the heat and serve.

CARMELA'S TIP:
- Dandelions do not last well once picked, so I would urge you to use them within a few hours of picking them.

Florentine Baked Pancakes,
Crespelle alla Fiorentina

Pancakes with a classic filling, topped with a simple béchamel and baked. This is a dish that hold simple yet joyful memories from my childhood. My mother Solidea would make this dish look effortless as she prepared it in a very methodical and precise manner. There are a few elements but as long as you can make pancakes then you'll be okay. I, however, am the worst pancake-maker out there and I should receive an award for this. I tend to leave that particular job to my husband, James.

Serves: 4
Preparation time: 30 minutes
Cooking time: 25 minutes

For the pancakes (*crespelle*)
2 eggs
250ml full-fat or semi-skimmed milk
100g '00' flour
60g salted butter, melted, plus extra for frying
salt and freshly ground black pepper

For the filling (*ripieno*)
300g spinach
250g ricotta
60g Pecorino Romano, grated
1 egg yolk
¼ tsp grated nutmeg

For the tomato sauce (*sugo*)
2 tbsp extra virgin olive oil
1 small shallot, finely chopped
1 garlic clove, crushed
350g tomato passata
small bunch of basil leaves, torn

For the béchamel sauce
500ml full-fat milk
50g salted butter
50g '00' flour
freshly grated nutmeg, to taste

For the topping
small bunch of basil
80g Pecorino Romano, grated

1. To make the batter, put the eggs and milk in a bowl and whisk to combine. Gradually add the flour, whisking continuously, to form a smooth batter. Stir in the melted butter, season with salt and pepper, cover and place in the fridge for at least 30 minutes.
2. Preheat the oven to 190°C fan (410°F/gas 6).
3. While the batter is in the fridge, prepare the filling. Blanch the spinach briefly then drain and squeeze out any excess water. Chop the spinach and place it in a bowl along with the ricotta and grated Pecorino. Stir to fully combine, then add the egg yolk, season with salt and pepper and sprinkle in the nutmeg. Taste and adjust the seasoning as required.
4. Take the pancake mixture out of the fridge. Grease a crêpe pan or regular frying pan with a little melted butter and make the pancakes as follows: place the pan over a medium heat, and when hot add a small ladle of batter. Tilt the pan so the base is evenly coated in the mixture, then cook for a minute or two until golden brown underneath. Flip over and cook the other side for another minute or so and transfer to a plate. Repeat until all the batter has been used up. The mixture should make 8 pancakes.
5. Now make the tomato sugo. Heat the oil in a small pan over a medium-low heat, add the shallot and fry gently for 10 minutes until translucent, then add the garlic and tomato passata. Season with salt and pepper and cook for 20 minutes. Add the torn basil and set aside.
6. To make the béchamel, warm the milk in a medium saucepan. Melt the butter in a separate small saucepan over a low heat, spoon in the flour and mix to form a roux. Cook the flour for a few minutes, stirring vigorously, then gradually add the milk to the roux, whisking slowly, and cook for 5–10 minutes until the

béchamel thickens slightly. Season with salt, pepper and a pinch of grated nutmeg. Remove from the heat and allow to cool at room temperature.

7. To assemble the dish, spoon and spread an even amount of the filling onto each pancake. Fold each pancake in half and then half again, making 8 envelopes.

8. Spoon a ladle of béchamel into a large oven dish, enough to cover the base of the dish with a thin layer of the white sauce. Lay each pancake onto the base of the dish. Sprinkle over the basil leaves and spoon on the rest of the béchamel. Add a layer of the tomato sugo and a heavy grating of Pecorino cheese.

9. Bake in the oven for 20–25 minutes until mildly golden and bubbling. Serve immediately.

CARMELA'S TIP:
• If you have any tomato sugo leftover, store it in the fridge for up to 5 days and use it in another recipe (or freeze it).

Gorgonzola and Ricotta Cavatelli,
Gorgonzola cavatelli

I have chosen to showcase a sauce from Gorgonzola, Lombardy, with pasta from the southern plains of Italy because this is a true reflection of how I like to cook and eat. Simple pasta with a complex, rich, yet moreish sauce. It produces a balance of flavour with perfectly poised and rolled ricotta cavatelli. Gorgonzola is a wonderful salty, crumbly cheese with distinctive greenish-blue veins running through it – it is effortless to eat. I also opt to use the slightly sweeter relation of the gorgonzola, dolcelatte; this cousin is milder and creamier, with a gentle sweetness.

Serves: 4
Preparation time: 1 hour 15 minutes (including resting and forming)
Cooking time: 20 minutes
You will need: a cavatelli maker (optional)

2 eggs
450g ricotta
400g '00' flour, plus extra for dusting
50g semola, for dusting
2 tbsp extra virgin olive oil
1 large shallot, thinly sliced
2 garlic cloves, crushed
300ml double cream
150g gorgonzola or dolcelatte
2 tbsp chopped parsley
60g Pecorino Romano, grated
salt and freshly ground black pepper

1. To make the ricotta cavatelli, mix the eggs with the ricotta in a bowl. Tip the flour onto a wooden board or a clean work surface, make a well in the middle and add the ricotta and egg mixture. Incorporate the ingredients with your hands until you have a smooth, pliable dough. Cover the dough and allow it to rest at room temperature for at least 20 minutes.
2. To form the cavatelli, roll out the dough and use a cavatelli maker

to make the pasta. Alternatively, cut the dough into 10 balls. Roll each ball into a long, thin rope that's around the thickness of a pen, then cut the ropes into 3cm-long pieces. Place a 3cm cavatelli piece onto a gnocchetti board, sushi mat or the back of a flat grater and, using a plain kitchen knife, place the knife in front of the cavatelli and, use a dragging motion to push the dough down the board, forming small ridges externally. Continue with the rest of the dough. Place all of the formed cavatelli onto a tray that has been dusted with semola. Allow to rest uncovered while you prepare the sauce.

3. Heat the olive oil in a shallow sauté pan over a medium heat, add the shallot and fry for 6 minutes until translucent and soft (don't let it colour). Add the garlic, stir and cook for 2 minutes then reduce the heat to low and pour in the cream. Stir and add the gorgonzola or dolcelatte cheese, either crumbled or whole, as it will melt into the pearly white cream regardless. Season with salt and pepper, going steady with the salt as the cheese is salty, and remembering to taste. Cook for 10 minutes over a low heat, ensure the mixture doesn't catch and burn at the bottom of the pan.

4. Bring a large 5-litre pan of water to the boil for the cavatelli. Once boiling, salt the water well, add the cavatelli and cook for 4 minutes until al dente.

5. Drain the pasta, reserving a small ladle of pasta water. Put the pasta back into the pan and dress it with the gorgonzola sauce.

6. Sprinkle over the parsley and half of the Pecorino. Stir to combine and serve in warm bowls with an extra grating of Pecorino.

Green Sauce, *Salsa verde*

Drizzle this sauce liberally over pan-fried fish, seasonal roasted vegetables or tagliata (sliced) steak. Salsa verde finishes off a dish with a crowning glory of freshness and sharply intense flavour. Adjust it to suit – if you prefer a little more lemon, then add it. I adore anchovies so I always add plenty of them because they offer such a natural saltiness. Choose herbs from your garden that are delicate and soft, remembering to change the herb combination with the change of season.

Serves: 4
Preparation time: 10 minutes

> small bunch of basil, finely chopped (including stems)
> small bunch of parsley, finely chopped (including stems)
> small bunch of mint, finely chopped (including stems)
> 1 large tbsp salted capers, rinsed well and patted dry
> 6 anchovy fillets (in oil), roughly chopped
> about 100ml extra virgin olive oil
> 3 tbsp fresh lemon juice, or to taste
> salt and freshly ground black pepper

1. Put the herbs and capers in a mortar and pound with a pestle for a few minutes, or blitz for 10 seconds in a mini food processor. Add the chopped anchovy fillets, along with half of the extra virgin olive oil, then blitz or pound for 20 seconds.
2. Scrape the ingredients together and stir, then gradually add the lemon juice and remaining oil until the salsa has a fresh yet relatively loose dropping consistency.
3. Season with salt and pepper, tasting and adjusting as required. Remember, this sauce should be sharp, with a fresh finish.

CARMELA'S TIP:
- You can prepare the salsa verde up to one day in advance.

Italian get-well soup, *Stracciatella*

Food can trigger memories, good and bad, from childhood to present day alike. Food, whether sweet or savoury – its aroma, its texture – can truly give us an instant sense of comfort and warmth that we sometimes don't even realise that we require. I have called this dish 'get-well soup', but in truth, whenever you need a speedy warming soup and have stock to hand (fresh, homemade stock is best here) then stracciatella is most definitely what I'd make. And you can tear up some slightly stale bread and dip it into the scrambly, loose mixture, too. As I sit here in my pasta room writing, I'm salivating and smiling as the memories from childhood come flooding back to me. Time to make stracciatella for lunch.

Serves: 2 (multiply as required)
Preparation time: 5 minutes
Cooking time: 8 minutes

650ml homemade chicken or vegetable stock (a good supermarket stock
or cube will suffice)
1 garlic clove, peeled, left whole
small bunch of parsley, chopped
4 eggs
grated zest of 1 small lemon and 2 tbsp lemon juice
1 tbsp finely chopped celery leaves
90g Parmigiano-Reggiano, freshly grated
salt and freshly ground black pepper
rustic bread, to serve

1. Bring your stock to a simmer in a saucepan over a medium heat then add the whole garlic clove to the stock along with half of the chopped parsley.
2. Beat the eggs in a bowl and season with salt and pepper.
3. Turn up the heat under the stock so it's simmering and pour in the egg. Allow the egg to cook for 30 seconds, without stirring, then, using a fork, separate and shred the eggy mixture into long strands.

4. Remove from the heat and add the lemon zest and juice. Sprinkle in the remaining parsley, celery leaves and grated Parmigiano.
5. Serve the soup in warmed bowls with extra black pepper and some rustic bread.

Ligurian Basil Pesto, *Pesto alla Genovese*

An essential verdant, textured dressing from the region of Liguria.
Made fresh, this pesto is the most versatile gift from the kitchen.
Spread onto warm toasted bread and top with roasted peppers and
speck, spooned and tossed through trofie pasta or drizzled over
oven-roasted vegetables. The choices are simply endless. A few
house rules, however, do apply: pesto should never be heated up as a
sauce on the hob – it is a fresh dressing; a pestle and mortar is the
traditional tool to make this pesto, and I do love tradition, but a food
processor is fully acceptable and welcomed with open arms when a
substantial quantity is required.

Makes: about 100g
Preparation time: 10 minutes
You will need: a small sterilised jar (if not using straight away) (see
page 9 for sterilising instructions)

25g untoasted pine nuts
1 garlic clove, peeled
125g fresh basil leaves
50g Parmigiano-Reggiano, grated
40ml extra virgin olive oil, plus extra if storing in a jar
salt and freshly ground black pepper

1. Using a pestle and mortar, pound the pine nuts and garlic
    together until they form a textured paste.
2. Add half of the basil leaves and crush with the pestle, combining
    them with the paste, then add the remaining basil leaves and
    crush them too.
3. Spoon in the grated Parmigiano and stir.
4. Slowly pour in the extra virgin olive oil, stirring to form a loose
    paste. Season to taste with salt and pepper.
5. Transfer the pesto to a sterilised jar (if not using immediately),
    top with extra virgin olive oil, seal and pop into the fridge. It will
    keep for about 3 weeks. Just remember, no double dipping!

CARMELA'S TIPS:
- Use a Ligurian extra virgin olive oil for pesto as it has a milder flavour.
- To make wild garlic pesto, make the pesto as above, substituting half the basil leaves for wild garlic leaves. I would not suggest a 100 per cent wild garlic pesto, as it would be too bitter.

Ligurian Focaccia, *Focaccia di Liguria*

This is an easy bread to master, and it offers an array of possibilities in term of toppings, from sprigs of verdant rosemary and sage to peeled tomatoes, chopped olives, caramelised onions, garlic or cheese. Or all of the above. The important thing is to achieve a lovely soft, fluffy bread. Once a focaccia has been made and cooled, I slice it in half lengthways, spoon in a layer of pesto followed by cured meat, roasted pepper and torn mozzarella with basil leaves, then slice and share.

Makes: 1 loaf
Preparation time: 10 minutes, plus 1 hour 30 minutes resting time
Cooking time: about 25 minutes

500g '00' flour, plus extra for dusting
7g sachet of fast-action dried yeast
1 tsp flaked sea salt (I use Maldon)
350ml tepid water
tbsp extra virgin olive oil
rock salt, for sprinkling
a few rosemary sprigs

1. Tip the flour into a mixing bowl. Add the yeast to one side of the bowl and the salt to the other.
2. Make a well in the centre of the flour and gradually add the water along with 4 tablespoons of the olive oil, stirring the liquid into the flour with your hands. Incorporate the oil and water into the flour until the mixture forms a dough and knead for 6–8 minutes.
3. Cover the dough with a clean tea towel and leave to rise at room temperature for about 1 hour, or until the dough has doubled in size. The time it takes to rise will vary, depending on the temperature of your kitchen.
4. After the dough has risen, knock it back and dust your work surface with flour. Roll it out to the size of the base of a baking sheet (about 25 x 35cm). Cover once again and leave at room temperature for a further 30 minutes to prove.
5. Preheat the oven to 220°C fan (475°F/gas 9).

6. Remove the cover from the focaccia. Use your fingertips to press random pits in the dough. Scatter over a little rock salt, a few sprigs of rosemary and drizzle over the remaining oil. Bake in the oven for about 25 minutes, until golden.

7. Remove from the oven and leave to cool for 10 minutes before placing the bread on a cooling rack to fully cool. Ideally eat it on the day it is made. Alternatively, it can be warmed up over the next few days, as required.

CARMELA'S TIP:
- If you have mozzarella water to hand, add it to the dough along with extra tepid water to top it up to 350ml.

Milanese Risotto, *Risotto alla Milanese*

Thank you, Milan, for this classic and stylish risotto: it's golden in colour and as stylish as you'd expect for a dish from this city. This *risotto alla Milanese* uses stunning saffron from L'Aquila in Abruzzo, and is well known as the base for the mouth-watering veal ossobuco (page 185). Feel free to use a vegetable stock instead of chicken and use a vegetarian hard cheese to make an easy vegetarian risotto. This amber risotto makes the most wonderful base for arancini – the classic Sicilian street food – too.

Serves: 4
Preparation time: 5 minutes
Cooking time: 30 minutes, plus resting time

1 litre chicken stock
2 tbsp extra virgin olive oil
70g salted butter
1 large shallot, thinly sliced
pinch of saffron strands
300g carnaroli risotto rice
150ml dry white wine or vermouth
80g Parmigiano-Reggiano, grated, plus extra to serve
small bunch of parsley, finely chopped
salt and freshly ground black pepper

1. Warm the stock in a saucepan and adjust the seasoning as required.
2. Heat the oil in a shallow sauté pan over a low heat and add 30g of the butter. Add the shallot and cook for 8 minutes until it has softened without colouring.
3. Put the saffron strands in a small heatproof bowl and add 2 tablespoons of the stock to awaken the saffron.
4. Add the rice to the sauté pan and toast it, stirring, for 1 minute, then add the white wine or vermouth and allow it to evaporate. Add a ladle of the hot stock to the rice and stir until it has been absorbed, then add the saffron along with the amber liquid. Continue adding the stock, a ladle at a time, stirring with a

wooden spoon that has a hole in the centre (if you have one) and letting each addition be absorbed before adding more.

5. Cook for about 18 minutes until the rice is cooked and al dente. Season to taste with salt and pepper.

6. Take the risotto off the heat and add the remaining butter, along with the Parmigiano and parsley. Stir well, cover the pan with a clean tea towel and clamp on a lid. Leave the risotto to rest for 5–10 minutes, then taste and add more seasoning if needed.

7. Serve the risotto with a little extra Parmigiano.

Passatelli in Stock, *Passatelli in brodo*

Passatelli: is it a pasta or an extruded, coarse bread dumpling? To me, of course, it's pasta and rightly so. I welcome the dish with warm memories of Nonna Violante from Romagna, who taught me the skill of making them, and a rumbling belly that anticipates eating them. The passatelli vary depending on whether bone marrow or stock is added to the dough, and the recipe uses lots of nutmeg, black pepper and sometimes lemon zest. Passatelli are simple to make, echoing the basic cooking from central Italy, and are awoken with a fantastic stock and the light touch of a skilful pasta maker, making them a standout dish on any dinner table.

Serves: 4
Preparation time: 30 minutes (including resting time)
Cooking time: 5 minutes
You will need: a potato ricer with holes at least 5mm in diameter (larger than a standard potato ricer), or a traditional passatelli press

400g stale breadcrumbs
200g Parmigiano-Reggiano, grated, plus extra to serve
3 eggs
50g '00' flour (if required) grated zest of ½ lemon (optional)
1 tsp freshly grated nutmeg
1.3 litres chicken or beef stock (preferably homemade)
salt and freshly ground black pepper

1. Put the breadcrumbs and Parmigiano on a wooden board or clean work surface. Stir with your hands to combine and make a well in the centre.
2. Crack the eggs into the centre of the well. Add the lemon zest (if using), nutmeg and season with salt and pepper.
3. Using a fork, slowly incorporating the eggs into breadcrumb mixture. Using your hands, work the mixture to form a dough and knead it for 3 minutes. If the dough is a bit wet (tacky), add a little '00' flour until the dough comes together; if the dough is dry, then add a little tepid water.
4. Place the dough in a clean bowl, cover the bowl with cling film and allow to rest at room temperature for at least 20 minutes.
5. Bring the stock to the boil in a large saucepan while you prepare the passatelli pasta.
6. Cut the dough into small workable sections then press each section of dough through the passatelli press or potato ricer, cutting them with a sharp knife when they are 4cm long. Lay them with care on a clean tea towel and continue until you have used all of the dough.
7. Reduce the heat so the stock is simmering, not boiling (a high heat would break up the passatelli), then add the passatelli to the stock and cook for 3 minutes. Ladle into warm bowls, scatter with extra Parmigiano and fall in love.

CARMELA'S TIPS:
- When making passatelli, it is essential that the breadcrumbs are stale and the bread contains a limited amount of oil (ideally none) as this will affect the overall cooking of the passatelli, making them temperamental and more likely to fall apart.
- If you are using beef stock, I would recommend you leave out the lemon zest.

Piadina (flatbread), *la piadina Romagnola*

Bread is almost as important to an Italian as the main meal itself. Piadina fills me with memories of Romagna. It is, in essence, a flatbread that is filled and eaten with a large smile and with gusto. I always like to scrape my bowl clean with a slice of bread or a piadina; equally, you could fill the piadina with roasted peppers, cured meats and cheeses and enclose the filling as you would wrap a newborn baby. Bread offers sustenance and can be paired with many a dish.

Serves: 4–6 (makes 6 piadine)
Preparation time: 30 minutes, plus 1 hour resting time
Cooking time: 4–10 minutes

500g '00' flour, plus extra for dusting
125g Italian lard (strutto), at room temperature
15g salt (I use Maldon)
1 tsp bicarbonate of soda
170ml water, at room temperature

1. Put the flour in a large bowl. Spoon in the lard, salt and bicarbonate of soda and stir well.
2. Gradually add the water and mix to form a dough. Tip the dough onto a clean work surface and knead for 5 minutes until smooth and elastic.
3. Put the dough in a bowl, cover the bowl with a clean tea towel or cling film and leave the dough to rest at room temperature for 30 minutes.
4. After 30 minutes, cut the dough into 6 portions and form each portion into a ball.
5. Cover once again and allow to rest at room temperature for a further 30 minutes.
6. Lightly dust a work surface with flour, then roll each ball of dough into a disc measuring 22cm in diameter.

7. Heat a large dry frying pan over a medium heat, then cook the piadinas one at a time for 2 minutes on each side, until the piadina catches a little colour, transferring them from the pan to a plate and covering them with a clean tea towel when cooked.
8. Fill and enjoy. I love mine with stracchino cheese and roasted vegetables. The piadina are best eaten on the day they are made, however you can keep them for a few days and simply soften them by warming them in a moderate oven for a few minutes.

Chickpea Balls, *Polpettine di ceci*

These chickpea balls are incredibly quick and easy to make, and are a blessing for the purse strings, too. For diversity of taste, allow the seasonal changes and abundance of herbs and vegetables to guide you when it comes to varying the flavour of the chickpea balls: add wild garlic during April and May, or a squeeze of lemon and a finely chopped courgette flower in the summer, perhaps. I like to serve mine dropped into a tomato sugo with extra seasoning and soft fresh herbs.

Makes: about 16 balls
Preparation time: 40 minutes (including chilling time)
Cooking time: 25 minutes

400g tin of chickpeas, drained (keep the water from the tin – see Tip)
80g Parmigiano-Reggiano, grated (or a vegetarian substitute)
50g stale breadcrumbs, plus extra for rolling
1 garlic clove, peeled and halved
1 egg
pinch of dried chilli flakes
½ tsp dried marjoram
small bunch of parsley, roughly chopped
small bunch of basil, roughly chopped
2 tbsp celery leaves
salt and freshly ground black pepper
olive oil, for frying (optional)

1. Put all of the ingredients, except the olive oil, in a food processor and pulse for 1 minute.
2. Using a spatula, scrape the contents of the processor into a clean bowl, stir, and season to taste.
3. Pinch off pieces of the mixture and roll into balls about the size of a small walnut.
4. Use all of the mixture – there should be enough for about 16 balls – then roll each ball in extra breadcrumbs to give each ball a protective coat. Pop the balls onto a tray and chill in the fridge for 30 minutes before cooking.

5. Cooking the chickpea balls:

Option 1 – Fry the chickpea balls in a little olive oil for about 10 minutes until lightly coloured. At this point the chickpea balls can be cooled and frozen.

Option 2 – Preheat the oven to 180°C fan (400°F/gas 6). Place the chickpea balls on a small baking tray and bake with a spritz of a spray cooking oil and bake for 25 minutes until lightly golden. These also freeze well.

CARMELA'S TIPS:

- Simply double the ingredients as required, so you have some for the freezer (freeze them cooked, not raw), or to increase the portions for main meals.
- Retain the aquafaba (chickpea water) from the tin as it makes wonderful vegan meringues, or use it to make pasta, bread or pizza dough.

Rigatoni with Guanciale, Pecorino and Black Pepper, *Pasta alla gricia*

From Lazio with love. *Pasta alla gricia* is the foundation for many of the well-known dishes that are born from this region, such as carbonara and amatriciana. Master this simple dish – a quick meal made using dried pasta, a little guanciale (pig's cheek) and Pecorino. Please always bear in mind that because it uses only a few ingredients, the quality of those ingredients is essential. That said, if you struggle to find guanciale then feel free to use a smoked pancetta instead.

Serves: 4
Preparation time: 5 minutes
Cooking time: 12 minutes

400g rigatoni
1 tbsp extra virgin olive oil
325g guanciale, cubed
100g Pecorino Romano, grated, plus 25g to serve (optional)
salt and freshly ground black pepper

1. Bring a large saucepan of water to the boil for the pasta. Once it's boiling, salt it well.
2. Cook the pasta following the packet instructions but cooking it for 2 minutes less so it is al dente.
3. Heat the oil in a frying pan over a low heat, add the guanciale and fry gently for 8 minutes or so, until golden.
4. Drain the pasta, reserving a ladle of the pasta water.
5. Tumble the pasta back into the pan and add the guanciale, along with the pecorino, and stir, adding some of the reserved pasta water in a steady stream to emulsify the sauce as you go.
6. Add a generous grind of black pepper and serve in warm bowls with the rest of the Pecorino (optional).

Rye Bread Soup, *Zuppa di pane nero*

Fresh rye bread that has been left to go stale is called for here. The rye, torn or shredded and steeped in a rich, warm, deep and reassuringly decadent beef stock, makes a soup that is almost heady in aroma, and so comforting. The chives add a sweet, savoury onion scent. Serve in warm bowls with an optional drizzle of extra virgin olive oil and a snowfall of grated Parmigiano.

Serves: 4
Preparation time: 10 minutes
Cooking time: 15 minutes

1 litre good-quality beef stock
300g small stale rye loaf, torn into bite-sized pieces
1 tbsp extra virgin olive oil
small bunch of chives, finely chopped
60g Parmigiano-Reggiano (or another preferred hard cheese), grated
salt and freshly ground black pepper

1. Bring the beef stock up to a steady simmer in a saucepan. Taste and check the stock, adding seasoning if necessary.
2. Scatter the bread into four warmed bowls.
3. Add a ladle of hot stock over each bowl of bread and finish with a drizzle of the olive oil, a sprinkle of chopped chives and a scattering of grated Parmigiano.

Snails with Tomatoes and Cocktail Sticks,
Lumache alla Romana

This is a beautifully simple dish, but one that requires an open mind. Growing up on a farm, my sister and I would go in search of snails so we could race them in 'monkey island', on a fallen tree trunk. My sister, however, would often love them a little too much: *crunch* goes the shell, ending the race prematurely. The adult in me now tolerates the dish as a sharing bowl, offered up with an espresso cup full of cocktail sticks and an empty bowl to catch the shells. The secret to a tender snail is to buy well, clean them thoroughly and cook them for a good few hours until tender. Here, I have chosen to celebrate them in a dish from Rome, made with tomatoes, anchovies and mint.

Serves: 4
Preparation time: 10 minutes
Cooking time: 2 hours 30 minutes
You will need: cocktail sticks

3 tbsp extra virgin olive oil
1 shallot, thinly sliced
1 garlic clove, thinly sliced
1 small fresh red chilli, deseeded and finely chopped
3 anchovy fillets (in oil), finely chopped
400g tin of plum tomatoes or 6 large seasonal plum tomatoes, peeled
(see Tip on page 67)
400g snails, cleaned
8 fresh mint leaves, thinly sliced
salt and freshly ground black pepper
bread, to serve

1. Heat the oil in a shallow saucepan over a medium heat, add the shallot and fry gently for 5 minutes until translucent but not coloured. Add the garlic, chilli and anchovy fillets, stir and fry over a low heat for 5 minutes until the anchovy fillets have disintegrated.

2. Increase the heat to medium and stir in the tomatoes, using the back of your wooden spoon to break them up a little. Season with a little salt and pepper.
3. Tumble in the snails and add half the mint leaves. Stir and cook over a low heat, covered with a lid, for 2 hours 30 minutes. If the pan is drying out, add a little water.
4. Check for seasoning once again, then add the remaining mint leaves and serve in a large bowl with a basket of bread for dipping and *per fare la scarpetta* (to scrape the bowl).

CARMELA'S TIP:

- If you are going to be frugal and hunt for snails, then be sure to purge them first and wash and clean them thoroughly: keep them in a large box with air holes, feed them on lettuce and carrots for a week, so that you know what they have eaten – this clears them out. Alternatively, you can starve them for a week. Be aware that snails pass a lot of poo. Wash them thoroughly once purged, then refrigerate the snails for at least 12 hours so they fall asleep before cooking as required.

Spaghetti Frittata, *Fritata di spaghetti*

This is not overly northern in terms of regionality, but pasta is pasta, and leftovers require a little guidance sometimes. I lose track of the number of students of mine who say that they always cook too much, in terms of quantity, when it comes to pasta. Now that leftover pasta can be made into another meal. You can transform pasta into many variations with a basic frittata recipe. This is divine for lunchboxes, snacks or a light lunch.

Serves: 4
Preparation time: 5 minutes
Cooking time: 10 minutes

6 eggs
70g Parmigiano-Reggiano, grated
2 tbsp finely chopped parsley
½ tsp dried marjoram
1 tbsp extra virgin olive oil
150g speck, roughly torn
400g leftover spaghetti
salt and freshly ground black pepper
dressed salad leaves or panino, to serve

1. Crack the eggs into a bowl and whisk. Add the Parmigiano, chopped parsley and marjoram and season with salt and pepper.
2. Heat the olive oil in a frying pan (about 26cm wide) over a low heat, add the torn speck and fry for 3 minutes until just coloured. The aroma is ridiculously pleasing right now, I'm sure you'll agree.
3. Add the spaghetti to the eggs and mix well. Pour the mixture into the frying pan and stir. Allow the frittata to settle and cook on the base for 3–5 minutes, then use a spatula to loosen the sides of the frittata. Place a dinner plate on top of the frittata and flip it over. Slide the frittata back into the pan and cook for a further 5–7 minutes.
4. Remove from the heat, slice and serve with dressed leaves. If I'm totally honest, I'd eat it squashed into a panino. The frittata can be served hot or cold and will keep in the fridge for up to 5 days.

Tomino Cheese Baked with Speck and Basil, *Tomino nel forno con speck e basilico*

Tomino is a soft cow's milk cheese with an edible rind and soft centre. If you've never tried this Piedmont treasure before, then please be sure to search it out and have a taste – you will fall in love instantly. Wrapping the tomino in a little speck protects the soft tomino body while the speck has the chance to turn a little crispy and slightly burnished, forming a firmer outer shell. This makes the perfect starter, one per diner, or the ultimate light lunch with a little rustic bread.

Serves: 4
Preparation time: 5 minutes
Cooking time: 8–10 minutes

8 fresh basil leaves, plus extra to serve
4 tomino cheese rounds
8 slices of speck

To serve
rocket leaves
aged balsamic vinegar, for drizzling

1. Preheat the oven to 180°C fan (400°F/gas 6) and line a baking tray with baking parchment.
2. Place 2 basil leaves on top of each round of tomino cheese and wrap a slice of speck around each tomino, then take a second slice of speck and wrap it around the bare part of the tomino so it's completely wrapped.
3. Place the wrapped tomino on the lined baking tray and bake for 8–10 minutes. They will only take a short time to cook, so don't take your eyes off them as they can easily burst and ooze everywhere.
4. Remove from the oven and serve on a few rocket leaves, with a drizzle of aged balsamic and a few tender basil leaves.

CARMELA'S TIP:
- Tomino freezes well, so stockpile it when you get the chance.

Veal Scalloppine with Marsala,

Scaloppine di vitello al marsala

My love of veal is well documented. I buy and use British veal, and have now found a wonderful butcher who is so very attentive to my every meat-loving whim. I find veal to be a little sweeter and so much more pleasing on the palate in this dish than pork, beef or chicken, however, feel free to substitute the veal as required.

Serves: 4
Preparation time: 15 minutes
Cooking time: 30 minutes

600g veal, cut into 4 slices
3 tbsp '00' flour, seasoned with salt and pepper
3 tbsp extra virgin olive oil
60g salted butter
250g mixed mushrooms, washed and finely chopped
3 sprigs of lemon thyme
150ml marsala
1 tbsp red wine vinegar
250ml chicken stock (fresh or made with 1 stock cube)
salt and freshly ground black pepper

1. Lay the sliced veal on a sheet of baking parchment and top with another sheet. Take a meat-tenderising mallet or rolling pin and gently pound the meat, taking care not to tear or damage the veal. This will tenderise the meat. Dredge the veal slices in the seasoned flour and set aside.
2. Heat 2 tablespoons of the olive oil in a shallow sauté pan over a low heat along with half the butter, add the chopped mushrooms, 1 sprig of the thyme and a pinch of salt and cook for 5–10 minutes until browned.
3. Remove the mushrooms from the pan and set aside.
4. Add the remaining butter to the pan along with the remaining oil and fry the veal *scaloppine* over a medium heat for 3 minutes on each side until browned and cooked through. Remove the veal and set aside.

5. Add the marsala and vinegar to the pan, cook for 5 minutes, then add the stock and return the veal and mushrooms to the pan. Cook for a further 15 minutes until the sauce has reduced a little.
6. Season with salt and pepper and add a sprinkle of fresh thyme leaves from the remaining sprigs.

CARMELA'S TIP:
- Serve with polenta or tiny rosemary potatoes and rocket leaves.

Summer

Long, lazy summer days. Weekends off work with family and friends. The laughter of children and the aroma of outdoor cooking. A sizzling barbecue, the always-acceptable popping of a cork at midday, the overeating and, more importantly, the sharing of food and memory-making.

Summer brings with it strawberries that actually taste sweet, ooze juice and leave you eating an entire punnet without realising it, so it's obligatory that I recommended you try without question my strawberry and prosecco risotto, finishing with a cheeky shot of prosecco poured over before serving.

Filled courgette flowers have to be one of the most popular and longingly anticipated edible flowers of the year, both in Italy and in the UK. They can be filled with ricotta and anchovy, dipped in batter and fried or filled with ricotta and lemon zest, battered and fried, then drizzled with a ridiculous amount of borage honey, and courgette fritters make the perfect light lunch, stuffed into a panino or eaten as a snack on the run.

The huge abundance of tomatoes at this time of year should be embraced. Use them and love them. I also sun-dry and preserve some for autumn, giving me a distant but delicious memory of summer flavours when the season has passed. Remember that tomatoes should be kept out of the fridge, in a bowl at room temperature. Straight from a fridge, even the most delicious of tomatoes will have no flavour. If you grow your own, please retain the tomatoes' vines for future use – a fantastic frugal tip that add punches of flavour with no effort. Use the tomato vines in your sauces, stocks and soups as a herb, and when used, simply discard. You can freeze the vines and use them directly from the freezer when required. Also, check out the recipe on page 31 to make my tomato vine liqueur.

My last share for summer is to please eat and enjoy as many fresh figs as you can (without upsetting your tummy, obviously). In season, this fruit is simply sensational. Fresh figs are incredible eaten in their natural voluptuous state, however drizzled with honey or baked with gorgonzola they send my heart racing a little faster. If you're lucky enough to grow your own figs or know somebody who does, use the fig leaves to make my liqueur (homemade fig-leaf gin on page 24), or steep them in milk and cream and make panna cotta. They have an intense yet delicate fragrance and exemplify seasonality and *cucina povera*.

Abruzzese Lamb Kebabs, *Arrosticini*

This almost isn't really a recipe – the ingredients and instructions are minimal – but I am not embarrassed to include it as it is much loved throughout the region of Abruzzo, and it embraces outdoor dining and the summer season. These easy lamb kebab skewers often make an appearance at my barbecues with an abundance of seasonal salads and warm breads.

Serves: 4
Preparation time: 10 minutes, plus 1 hour (minimum) marinating
Cooking time: 10 minutes
You will need: 8 wooden skewers, soaked in water for 15 minutes

4 tbsp extra virgin olive oil
sprig of rosemary, needles finely chopped
1 plump garlic clove, peeled
650g lamb shoulder, diced
salt and freshly ground black pepper

To serve
bread
salad
aged balsamic vinegar

1. Pour the olive oil into a large bowl. Add the chopped rosemary and the garlic clove and season with salt and pepper. Add the diced lamb shoulder, stir to coat it in the oil, and leave at room temperature to marinate for at least 1 hour (up to 12 hours would be sensational, in which case marinate it in the fridge).
2. Get your barbecue and coals up to grilling temperature.
3. Drain the skewers and push the marinated lamb onto the skewers or prepared rosemary sticks (see Carmela's tip).
4. Cook the lamb skewers on the barbecue for 4 minutes, turning them regularly, and serve with bread, salad and a wonderfully aged balsamic vinegar.

CARMELA'S TIP:

- To make rosemary sticks, take 8 long sturdy sprigs of fresh rosemary. Remove the rosemary needles and set them aside for using in another recipe. Soak the rosemary 'skewers' in water for 15 minutes, then drain, add the meat and cook as above.

Artichokes filled with Taleggio,

Carciofi ripiene di Taleggio

Artichokes filled with fragrant basil, soft Taleggio and wrapped in a coat of salty speck. This is one of my favourite starters, not only because of its simplicity but also because using artichokes from a tin or jar means there's limited preparation. It isn't dependent on the seasons for the same reason. Perfect as a weekend snack or starter served with a wonderfully deep, aged balsamic vinegar. Dip me, fry me, eat me!

Serves: 6
Preparation time: 15 minutes
Cooking time: 20 minutes (as you will need to batch-cook them)

12 small artichoke hearts, from a jar or tin
12 large basil leaves
250g Taleggio, cut into 12 pieces
12 slices of speck or prosciutto
1 litre sunflower oil, for deep-frying
4 tbsp '00' flour
rocket leaves, to serve

For the batter
1 large egg white, beaten
140ml sparkling water
100g '00' flour
pinch of dried oregano
grated zest of 1 lemon (cut the zested lemon into wedges, to serve)

1. Drain the artichokes and pat them dry with kitchen paper. Handling them with care, use a teaspoon make a small hole in the centre of each artichoke.
2. Push a basil leaf into the base of each artichoke followed by a piece of soft Taleggio.
3. Wrap each artichoke firmly in a piece of speck, secure with a cocktail stick and leave to one side.

4. Heat the oil in a large high-sided saucepan to 190°C (375°F). If you don't have a thermometer to hand then simply drop in a small cube of bread – it should brown within 30 seconds.
5. To make the light batter, whisk the egg white and sparkling water together in a bowl, then add the flour and whisk until smooth. Season with salt, pepper and stir in the dried oregano and lemon zest.
6. Put the 4 tablespoons of flour in a shallow bowl. Coat 4 of the artichokes in the flour then dip them in the batter. Fry the artichokes for about 4 minutes until golden, remove with a slotted spoon and transfer to kitchen paper to absorb excess oil. Repeat this process with the remaining stuffed artichoke hearts.
7. Serve the fried artichokes on a platter with rocket leaves and lemon wedges.

Beef Carpaccio with Pink Pepper and Rocket, *Carpaccio di manzo*

When beef is cut wafer thin, dressed beautifully and presented centre-stage on your dining table, it is worthy of an award. Light, fragrant and reminiscent of many a summer holiday in Italy, this dish melts in the mouth. The trick is to firstly freeze the beef fillet to make the slicing effortless, and secondly to allow the meat to marinate at room temperature (not to serve the carpaccio directly from the fridge).

Serves: 4 as a starter
Preparation time: 20 minutes, plus 2 hours' freezing time

400g beef fillet
150g rocket leaves
80g Taggiasca olives
40g sun-dried tomatoes, roughly chopped
small bunch of basil leaves
salt and freshly ground black pepper
Parmagiano shavings, to serve

For the vinaigrette
100ml extra virgin olive oil
50ml lemon juice
20ml lime juice
15–20 pink peppercorns

1. For ease of slicing, place the beef fillet in the freezer for 2 hours.
2. Remove the beef from the freezer and, using a very sharp knife, cut it into wafer-thin slices. Lay the slices on a sheet of greaseproof paper. Lay another sheet of greaseproof paper on top and, very gently, without too much pressure, pound the beef slices with a rolling pin. Lay the beef slices over a large platter.
3. Combine the vinaigrette ingredients and a generous twist of salt and pepper in a small bowl.
4. Drizzle half of the prepared vinaigrette over the prepared beef and leave to rest at room temperature for 15 minutes.

5. Dress the rocket leaves with the remaining vinaigrette.
6. Scatter the rocket leaves over the beef and top with the dainty Taggiasca olives and sun-dried tomatoes.
7. Add the basil and shavings of Parmigiano.

CARMELA'S TIP:
*   Taggiasca olives are from the region of Liguria and are deliciously tiny, but feel free to use whatever you have to hand as these may not be available.

Cod with Sliced Prunes and Raisins,

Baccalà con prugne e uvetta

This dish of baccalà and fruit is very much loved and enjoyed in the northern regions of Italy, with Tuscany particularly embracing the combination of cod and prunes. I tend to cook baccalà in the run-up to the Christmas and festive period. My local Italian deli stocks the best salted baccalà over this period, and it always sells incredibly quickly. Baccalà doesn't need to live in the fridge as it's preserved in salt, so I tend to buy enough to see me through a few months and store it in an airtight container in my larder. Preparation and the soaking of the fish is key for the perfect execution of this dish.

Serves: 2
Soaking time: 2 days
Preparation time: 15 minutes
Cooking time: 25 minutes

500g baccalà (salt cod)
30g raisins
30ml warm vegetable stock
2 tbsp extra virgin olive oil
25g butter
1 large shallot, finely chopped
1 small celery stick, finely chopped
1 garlic clove, crushed
500g tomato passata
1 tbsp chopped celery leaves
30g pitted prunes, thinly sliced
a small handful of fennel fronds, finely chopped
freshly ground black pepper
rustic bread or soft polenta, to serve

1. Two days before serving, place the baccalá in a large bowl of cold water. Leave it to soak for 2 days in the fridge, discarding and replenishing the water every few hours to remove the salt and rehydrate the fish.

2. After two days' soaking, remove the salt cod from the liquid. Pat it dry and ensure it is bone-free, and set it aside for later.
3. Put the raisins in the vegetable stock for 15 minutes to plump up.
4. Heat the oil and butter in a large, shallow frying pan over a low heat, add the shallot and celery, increase the heat to medium and cook for about 10 minutes until softened. Add the garlic and stir, then pour in the tomato passata and add the celery leaves. Stir well.
5. Cut the baccalà into two pieces and lay it directly into the passata. Sprinkle over the prunes, raisins and stock. Stir gently, season with pepper, and cook uncovered for 15–20 minutes, uncovered. Taste for additional seasoning – you may at this point wish to add salt.
6. Remove from the heat, sprinkle with the fennel and serve with rustic bread or a little soft polenta.

Courgette Fritters, *Zucchini frittelle*

I am a courgette lover. You can fry them, bake them, slice and dress them raw with lemon, fill them, grate them. I have endless love for this vegetable, never mind the beautiful flower that it also produces (see page 72 for a great way to use these). Here, I give you my courgette fritters. Serve as a side dish, as a light lunch with salad, or layered into a panino with Genovese Pesto (page 5) and some roasted peppers. Forever hungry, forever eating.

Serves: 4
Preparation time: 10 minutes
Cooking time: 18 minutes

3 medium courgettes, coarsely grated
2 eggs, whisked
small handful of mint, finely chopped
small handful of parsley, finely chopped
80g Parmigiano-Reggiano, grated
grated zest and juice of 1 small lemon
70g '00' flour
4 tbsp light olive oil
salt and freshly ground black pepper

1. Squeeze out any excess liquid from the courgettes, put them in a mixing bowl and add the eggs. Stir to combine. Tumble in the chopped mint, parsley, Parmigiano, lemon zest and juice and stir again, then add the flour and mix to combine. Season with salt and pepper.
2. Heat the oil in a shallow sauté pan over a medium heat. Add a tablespoon of the fritter mixture at a time to the pan, pressing each spoonful down to form shallow discs (fry them in batches and avoid overcrowding the pan). Fry for 3 minutes, then carefully flip them over with a spatula and fry for a further 3 minutes until golden and crispy.
3. Remove the cooked *fritelle* from the heat and place on a plate lined with kitchen paper to remove any excess oil. Repeat with the remaining batter.

CARMELA'S TIP:
- I sometimes like to add a little crumbled gorgonzola or dolcelatte to the courgette mixture. Feta works incredibly well, too.

Egg and Courgette Roulade with Ricotta and Speck, *Rotolo di uova al ricotta e speck*

This rotolo is a weekly staple in my kitchen. It can be whatever you want it to be: part of your brunch, a light lunch, or part of your evening meal. It's totally adaptable. My *rotolo* is, in essence, a giant savoury Swiss roll. Once the rotolo base is cooled, I simply slice it (without filling) and have it for breakfast, as a snack or squashed in-between two slices of perfectly squishy bread, layered with chopped, jarred artichokes, roasted warm peppers and a few rocket leaves. Versatility meets simplicity.

Serves: 6
Preparation time: 10 minutes
Cooking time: 20 minutes, plus cooling
You will need: a baking tray or Swiss roll tin roughly 39 x 27cm (2cm deep)

For the rotolo
10 eggs
1 large courgette, grated and drained
grated zest of 1 lemon
60g Parmigiano-Reggiano, grated
1 small fresh red chilli, deseeded and finely chopped
1 tsp dried marjoram
2 courgette flowers, washed, internal bud removed,
and sliced lengthways (optional)
2 tbsp chopped parsley
2 tbsp chopped basil
salt and freshly ground black pepper

For the filling
250g ricotta
juice of 1 lemon
8 slices of speck
180g roasted red peppers, sliced
15 basil leaves

1. Preheat the oven to 180°C fan (400°F/gas 6) and line the baking tray with baking parchment.
2. Spoon the ricotta into a bowl and season it with salt and pepper.
3. Take a large bowl, crack in the eggs and whisk for 1 minute until well combined. Add the grated courgette, lemon zest, Parmigiano and chopped chilli and stir, then add the dried marjoram, courgette flowers (if using), parsley and basil. Mix and season with salt and pepper.
4. Add the lemon juice to the ricotta and stir.
5. Ladle the egg mixture into the lined Swiss roll tin and bake in the oven for 20 minutes.
6. Remove from the oven and leave for 10 minutes before turning the rotolo base out onto a wire rack.
7. Roll the rotolo lengthways (unfilled) and wrap in a tea towel to cool fully.
8. Unwrap the rotolo and spread over the ricotta filling, leaving a 1cm gap around the edges. Scatter over the roasted peppers and basil leaves.
9. Re-roll the rotolo then slice it into 3cm-thick pieces. Chill in the fridge until required. This can be made up to 3 days ahead and will keep for up to 6 days.

Fennel, Tomato and Thyme Bake,
Finocchio, pomodoro e timo gratinato

Whether prepared as a satisfying side or simply served on its own with some fresh bread, this bake is a gorgeous dish for summer. I make my *gratinato* a little juicier purely so the bread has the chance to absorb the wonderful sauce. Dipping your bread and scraping it lovingly over and in your sauce is called *'fare la scarpetta'* – it is, without fail, a perfect end-of-meal task. The baked fennel has wonderfully delicate aniseed notes, and when it's kissed with a little heat it mellows into a sweetness that is irresistible.

Serves: 4 as a side, or 2 as a main
Preparation time: 10 minutes
Cooking time: 50 minutes

4 tbsp extra virgin olive oil
1 banana shallot, thinly sliced
4 plump fennel bulbs, cut into wedges (retain the fronds for the topping)
3 garlic cloves, thinly sliced
25g salted capers, rinsed well and chopped
400g tin of cherry tomatoes
100ml vegetable stock
100g stale breadcrumbs
70g Parmigiano-Reggiano, grated
4 tbsp finely chopped fennel fronds
grated zest of 1 small lemon
30g pitted green olives, finely chopped
salt and freshly ground black pepper

1. Preheat the oven to 190°C fan (410°F/gas 6).
2. Heat 3 tablespoons of the olive oil in a shallow saucepan over a medium heat, add the shallots and fennel wedges and cook for 15 minutes until softened and lightly coloured.
3. Add the garlic and capers to the pan, followed by the cherry tomatoes and stock. Stir, season with salt and pepper, and cook for a further 15 minutes until the fennel is completely tender.

4. Put the breadcrumbs, Parmigiano, chopped fennel fronds, lemon zest and olives in a bowl, stir and season with salt and pepper. This will be the crowning glory.
5. Transfer the fennel and shallot into a shallow oven dish and top with the flavoured breadcrumb mix. Drizzle with the remaining tablespoon of olive oil and bake in the oven for 20 minutes until golden and tender.
6. Remove from the oven and serve.

Filled and Deep-fried Courgette Flowers,
Fiori di zucchini

I would sooner receive the gift of two or three courgette flowers
than a dozen red roses. I look forward to getting my hands on them
most of the year, from summer to summer. This season always
reminds me of my dad Rocco's allotment being overrun by
courgettes that all hold their own unique bud. Early in the courgette
season, the male courgette flowers appear on a stem that produces
no flower. Later in the season, the female flower is produced
bearing the courgette. On the inside, each flower is a little different,
with the male flower housing a single stamen, while the more
voluptuous flower from the female have a slightly more complex
interior. Irrespective of sex, remove the centre buds and stamens of
both flowers and prepare them for filling.

Serves: 4
Preparation time: 15 minutes
Cooking time: 15 minutes
You will need: a piping bag (optional)

For the filling
250g ricotta
1 egg yolk
4 anchovy fillets (in oil), finely chopped
grated zest and juice of 1 small lemon
leaves from 4 sprigs of marjoram and thyme
½ tsp dried oregano
1 litre sunflower or light olive oil, for deep-frying
8 courgette flowers, washed and internal buds removed
salt and freshly ground black pepper

For the batter
1 egg white
4 tbsp '00' flour
1 tbsp lemon juice
30ml sparkling water, at room temperature

1. Put the ricotta and egg yolk in a medium bowl and stir with a spatula to combine.
2. Add the chopped anchovy fillets, lemon zest and some of the lemon juice (retaining 1 tablespoon of the lemon juice for the batter). Mix well. Add the marjoram and thyme leaves and the dried oregano and season with salt and pepper. Taste and adjust seasoning as required.
3. I like to spoon the mixture into a piping bag for ease, but of course you can use a teaspoon if you prefer. Secure the top of the bag with a clip and set aside.
4. Heat the oil into a large high-sided saucepan to 190°C (375°F).
5. While it heats up, prepare the batter. Whisk the egg white in a clean bowl until fluffy. Fold in the flour and stir, add the lemon juice and sparkling water. Whisk to incorporate and ensure the batter is lump free. Season with salt and pepper.
6. Fill the cavity of each courgette flower with the ricotta filling, leaving a couple of centimetres at the top so that you are able to twist the petals together and secure the top of the flower. Repeat with all the flowers.
7. Test the oil has reached the right temperature by dropping in a little bread: if the bread browns within 30 seconds, the oil is ready. Line a tray with a few sheets of kitchen paper.
8. Dip two or three filled *fiori di zucchini* into the batter, then gently shake off any excess.
9. Carefully lay the flowers in the oil and fry for 3 minutes until cooked, ensure you turn to cook them on all sides. (Cooking them in batches avoids overcrowding the pan and the oil temperature dropping.) Remove with a slotted spoon and place on the lined tray.
10. Repeat with remaining stuffed flowers and eat immediately.

CARMELA'S TIP:
- I sometimes use half sparkling water and half milk in the batter. It makes a light batter that also helps tenderise firmer vegetables, so is useful if you make fritto misto.

Filled Cavolo Nero Leaves,

Cavolo nero ripiene (capuns)

This dish encompasses the richness of the cuisine of north Italy with the simplistic *cucina povera* qualities from the south. This dish has roots in Switzerland and has been adopted by the mountain regions of Italy, adapted to taste and loved unconditionally. You can swap the cavolo nero leaves for kale or cabbage.

Serves: 4
Preparation time: 20 minutes
Cooking time: 35 minutes

20 cavolo nero leaves, washed thoroughly and tough stalks removed
2 tbsp extra virgin olive oil
30g salted butter
2 shallots, finely chopped
2 garlic cloves, crushed
300g firm Italian sausages, skins removed, meat finely chopped
50g '00' flour
2 eggs
250g ricotta
50g white bread, soaked in 2 tbsp milk for 10 minutes
70g Parmigiano-Reggiano, grated, plus extra to serve
4 tbsp chopped parsley
150ml double cream
100ml vegetable stock
6 slices of speck, cut into strips
salt and freshly ground black pepper

1. Heat the oil with the butter in a small frying pan over a low heat, tumble in the shallots and garlic and cook over a medium heat for 4 minutes. Add the chopped sausage meat to the pan and cook for 5 minutes until lightly browned.
2. Put the flour, eggs, ricotta, soaked bread and Parmigiano in a bowl and stir to form a loose batter and add the sausage mixture to the bowl.

3. Season with salt and pepper and add the chopped parsley. Stir to mix thoroughly and taste for any additional seasoning.
4. Place a tablespoon of the mixture into the centre of a cavolo nero leaf. Fold in the sides and then roll up the leaf, ensuring the filling is completely covered. Repeat with all of the filling and cavolo nero leaves.
5. Using a kitchen towel, wipe clean the frying pan and reuse. Pour the cream and stock into the frying pan and bring to a simmer over a medium heat. Season with a little salt and pepper.
6. Lay the filled cavolo nero rolls in the simmering sauce, cover and cook gently for about 25 minutes.
7. While the cavolo nero rolls are cooking, fry the sliced speck in a dry frying pan until golden and crispy.
8. Spoon the cavolo nero rolls into bowls with a ladle of the sauce and top with a dusting of grated Parmigiano and a small handful of crispy speck.

CARMELA'S TIP:
*   Add a little freshly chopped red chilli for warmth.

Fish in Crazy Water, *Pesce all'acqua pazza*

The mellow heat and chilli is said to make the water crazy, but years ago fishermen would cook this dish using sea water, hence the term *'crazy water'*. The dish is simple to put together but calls for the freshest whole fish you can get your hands on, as the broth benefits from the entire fish. Please do not be tempted to use fillets.

Serves: 2
Preparation time: 14 minutes
Cooking time: 20 minutes

100g fresh clams, scrubbed clean
600ml water
2 large garlic cloves, thinly sliced
15 cherry tomatoes, halved
1 small fresh chilli, deseeded and thinly sliced
small bunch of parsley, chopped (including stems)
2 whole bass or mullet (about 280g each), scaled, gutted and cleaned
125ml white wine or vermouth
salt and freshly ground black pepper

To serve
extra virgin olive oil, for drizzling
rustic bread
1 small lemon, quartered

1. Check the clams are all closed and that none of the shells are cracked, damaged or opened. If they are, then simply discard them.
2. Pour the water into a large, heavy-based shallow pan (one big enough to accommodate both fish, that has a lid). Place the pan on the hob and bring the water to a gentle simmer. Add the sliced garlic, halved cherry tomatoes, fresh chilli and the parsley stems and season with a little salt and pepper. Cook for 5 minutes over a medium heat and stir.
3. Lay the fish in the pan, top to tail.

4. Pour in the wine or vermouth and clamp on the lid. Leave for about 7 minutes, then lift the lid and, with care, flip the fish over and scatter in the clams.

5. Replace the lid and continue to cook for a further 7 minutes, until the fish is tender and cooked through and the clams have popped open.

6. If any clams remain unopened, please discard them. Taste the broth for additional seasoning before serving.

7. Place the fish on a deep-sided platter and add the cooking liquid and tomatoes. Scatter over the chopped parsley leaves and add a good drizzle of extra virgin olive oil, and serve with rustic bread and lemon wedges.

CARMELA'S TIP:

- When tomatoes are not at their best and in season, use a 400g tin of cherry tomatoes as an alternative. Ask your fishmonger to prepare you fish for you.

Green Bean Salad, *Fagolini al olio e limone*

This *fagolini* (green bean) salad can be found as a side at many, if not all, of my summer engagements. I often have it just on its own, dressed with a little grated Parmigiano. It's my daughter Natalia's favourite side dish – if she could have it daily, she would.

Serves: 4
Preparation time: 5 minutes
Cooking time: 5 minutes
Chilling and resting time: 1 hour

> 500g green beans, topped and tailed
> 2 garlic cloves, thinly sliced
> 3 tbsp extra virgin olive oil
> grated zest and juice of 1 small lemon
> 1 tbsp finely chopped parsley

1. Bring a saucepan of water to the boil and prepare a bowl of ice-cold water.
2. Salt the water, add the beans and cook for about 5 minutes until al dente.
3. When cooked, drain the beans, plunge them into the bowl of ice-cold water and leave them in the water for 30 minutes. This will stop the beans from cooking further and ensures that they hold their verdant colour.
4. Drain the beans from the cold water and place them on a serving dish.
5. Combine the garlic, oil, lemon zest and juice, and parsley in a small bowl.
6. Dress the beans and toss, then leave for 30 minutes at room temperature before serving.

CARMELA'S TIP:

- Scatter over some Italian pine nuts and add a little honeyed ricotta over the finished salad. I also like to roast some cherry tomatoes with oregano, then when they burst, I sprinkle them on top of the beans. There are endless possibilities.

Nonna Carmela's Fig with Gorgonzola, Speck, Walnuts and Honey,

Fico al gorgonzola e miele

I can still smell the aroma of the plump, green summer figs that Nonna Carmela passed to me in her tiny hands. Almost 91 years old, Nonna Carmela would say, in Italian, 'Have them, Carmelina. One for now and one for your journey home.' She understood my love for fresh figs, picked off her huge tree that spilled into her recently departed neighbour's garden. Nonna was always battling the thieving birds, so would wrap each fig in either a small plastic bag or in old stockings with the aim of protecting them, if only to save but a few. I am a fig purist when it comes to eating them when they are in season – they require nothing but a hungry Carmela. That said, I am only one woman, so even I require a little help in eating them. This recipe is a classic with a little twist, as I like to use speck instead of prosciutto.

Makes: 6 filled figs
Preparation time: 15 minutes
Cooking time: 25 minutes

6 plump, seasonal figs
200g gorgonzola
6–12 slices of speck
honey, for drizzling
30g salted butter
70g walnuts, chopped

1. Preheat the oven to 170°C fan (375°F/gas 5) and line a baking tray with baking parchment.
2. Slice into the top of each fig, making a cross, but do not cut down to the base. Squeeze each fruit gently to open up the cross.
3. Crumble gorgonzola into each cross then wrap each fig with a slice or two of speck. Place the figs on the lined baking tray, drizzle over a tiny amount of honey and bake in the oven for 25 minutes.

4. Meanwhile, melt the butter in a small frying pan over a medium heat, add the walnuts and fry for 5 minutes. Remove the pan from the heat and add a teaspoon of honey and stir.
5. Serve the figs in their crispy speck jackets on a slightly warmed platter. Sprinkle over the burnished walnuts and drizzle over a little more honey.

CARMELA'S TIP:
- Choose a seasonal or local honey. I currently have a love and fondness for borage honey.

Prosecco Risotto with Strawberries,

Risotto di prosecco e fregola

Take a simple plain, white risotto and pour in the freshness of prosecco bubbles from the town of Valdobbiadene, in the province of Treviso, Veneto, then pair it with the natural sweetness of ruby-red seasonal strawberries. This dish requires the sweetest of strawberries so please only make it during the British strawberry season, which is usually from mid-May to the end of September.

Serves: 4
Preparation time: 25 minutes
Cooking time: 30 minutes, plus resting time

350g strawberries, quartered
250ml prosecco
650ml vegetable stock
1 tbsp olive oil
60g salted butter
1 shallot, thinly sliced
1 garlic clove, crushed
350g vialone nano risotto rice
60g Parmigiano-Reggiano, grated
1 tbsp finely chopped mint leaves, plus extra to serve
salt and freshly ground black pepper

1. Put almost all the quartered strawberries in a bowl with 50ml of the processo and leave them to steep for 15 minutes.
2. Warm the stock in a saucepan, taste and check for seasoning, adjusting as necessary.
3. Heat the oil and 30g of the butter in a shallow sauté pan over a medium heat, add the shallot and fry for about 5 minutes until translucent, then add the garlic and cook for 2 minutes, stirring well.
4. Add the risotto rice to the pan and stir over a medium heat, coating the rice in the shallot mixture, and toast it for 1 minute, then add the prosecco and stir for 5 minutes or so, allowing the prosecco to evaporate.

5. Slowly begin to add the stock, one ladle at a time, stirring frequently with a wooden spoon that has a hole in the centre (if you have one), and cook for about 18 minutes until the rice is cooked and al dente. Season to taste with salt and pepper.
6. Strain the strawberries and reserve the prosecco for drinking.
7. Remove the risotto from the heat and add the Parmigiano and the rest of the butter. Stir well, cover the pan with a clean tea towel and clamp on a lid. Leave the risotto to rest for 5–10 minutes.
8. Add the chopped mint leaves and the Prosecco-steeped strawberries to the risotto and serve it on warmed plates with a scattering of fresh strawberries and tiny mint leaves.

CARMELA'S TIPS:
- Arborio or carnaroli rice are equally acceptable alternatives to vialone nano.
- As I serve each plate of risotto, I love to pour a shot of prosecco over the dish.

Saltimbocca, *Saltimbocca alla Romana*

Saltimbocca means to 'jump in my mouth'. 'Oh yes, please!' I say, with a rosy smile and rumbling tummy. This dish is a little showstopper, always well received thanks to the cocktail stick holding together three layers of flavour. This recipe makes plenty as they are just as delicious served cold, squashed into a late-night panino with a spoonful of pesto (page 52). Feel free to substitute the veal for pork if you prefer.

Serves: 4
Preparation time: 20 minutes
Cooking time: 20 minutes
You will need: cocktail sticks

8 veal escalopes
3 tbsp '00' flour, seasoned with salt and pepper
8 slices of prosciutto crudo or speck
12 large sage leaves
1 tbsp extra virgin olive oil
80g salted butter
125ml white wine

1. Dredge each slice of veal in the flour then lay each slice of veal out on a board.
2. Place a slice of prosciutto or speck on top of a slice of veal then add a token sage leaf to the top of the prosciutto. Secure and weave the veal, prosciutto and sage together with a cocktail stick to hold the layers in place. Repeat with the remaining veal and prosciutto.
3. Heat the oil and butter in a large, shallow sauté pan over a medium heat. Add the slices of saltimbocca sage side down and cook for 5 minutes then flip them over and add the white wine. Cook for a further 4 minutes or so. I like mine to have a firm, crisp top.
4. Transfer to a warm serving dish that has a lip. Spoon over the melted butter from the pan and serve.

CARMELA'S TIP:
- Serve alongside softened cavolo nero and some baby rosemary and garlic potatoes, or for lunch with a leaf salad.

Schiacciata with Cherry Tomatoes,
Schiacciata di pomodorini

A delicious Tuscan loaf with a dense yet perfectly acceptable thickness to it. Like many fresh breads, I find this one is best eaten fresh on the day. Leftover *schiacciata* can be warmed in the oven and eaten the following day.

Makes: 2 flat loaves
Preparation time: 20 minutes, plus 1 hour 30 minutes proving
Cooking time: 25 minutes
You will need: 2 x 24cm cake tins or two 20 x 40cm baking trays

220ml water, at room temperature
7g sachet of fast-action dried yeast
½ tbsp caster sugar
400g '00' flour, plus extra for dusting
40ml extra virgin olive oil or melted lard, plus extra oil for drizzling
13g salt (I use Maldon), plus extra for sprinkling
25 cherry tomatoes, halved (I like to use a mixture of red and yellow seasonal varieties)
½ tsp dried oregano or marjoram

1. Put the water in a jug or bowl, add the yeast and sugar, stir and leave for 15 minutes to activate.
2. Put the flour in a large bowl with the olive oil or lard, yeast and water mixture and salt. Stir using your hands until the mixture comes together to form a dough, then knead on a lightly floured work surface for about 8 minutes until smooth and elastic.
3. Transfer to a bowl, cover the bowl with cling film and allow the dough to rise at room temperature for 1 hour or until doubled in size.
4. Preheat the oven to 220°C fan (475°F/gas 9) and grease the cake tins or baking trays with olive oil.

5. Split the dough in half and form it into two flat discs measuring about 24cm in diameter. Push the dough into the greased cake tins or baking trays and rest at room temperature for 30 minutes, covered with a clean tea towel, until it has increased in volume by a third.

6. Decorate each loaf with the cherry tomatoes, with the cut sides facing down. Sprinkle over a little salt, a splash of water, a drizzle of olive oil, and the oregano or marjoram and bake for 25 minutes until golden.

7. Remove from the oven and cool. Eat on the same day.

Sliced T-bone with Balsamic Cherry Tomatoes, *Tagliata di manzo*

Tagliata means 'cut'. To me, a sliced cut of meat offered on a wooden board and placed in the centre of a table is a thing of sheer beauty. Serving your steak sliced into strips – whether it be a T-bone, sirloin, or rump – makes it tend to go further and feed more people too, especially when served with a variety of sides. It can also be effortless to put together. If I use a T-bone or two, I tend to keep hold of the bones once we have finished eating, and put them in a container before chilling or freezing them for making stock at a later date.

Serves: 4
Preparation time: 15 minutes, plus oil infusing time
Cooking time: 20 minutes

2 sprigs of rosemary
100ml extra virgin olive oil, plus an extra 2 tbsp for frying
1 medium shallot, thinly sliced
2 garlic cloves, crushed
450g cherry tomatoes, halved
1 tbsp capers in salt, drained, rinsed and roughly chopped
small bunch of basil leaves, roughly torn
2 x 600g T-bone or sirloin steaks (or your preferred cut)
1 tbsp aged balsamic vinegar
200g rocket leaves
70g Pecorino Romano or Parmigiano-Reggiano, grated (optional)
salt and freshly ground black pepper

1. Give the rosemary sprigs a gentle squeeze to release their aroma, put them in a bowl and cover with the 100ml olive oil. I tend to leave this to infuse for an hour, but you could gently warm the oil then add the rosemary sprigs and steep for 10 minutes if you're short on time.

2. Heat the remaining 2 tablespoons of oil in a small saucepan over a medium heat, add the shallot and fry gently for 6 minutes until the shallot just begins to colour. Add the garlic and halved cherry tomatoes to the pan, stir, add the capers and cook for 10 minutes before adding half the torn basil. Remove from the heat and season with salt and pepper.

3. Season each steak with salt and pepper on both sides. Use your fingers to rub the seasoning into the skin.

4. Using a rosemary sprig, paint each steak with a little of the infused oil.

5. Heat a large frying pan over a high heat, place the steaks in the pan and fry for about 4 minutes on one side, then turn them over and cook for a further 4 minutes. Adjust the cooking times according to the size of the steak, whether or not it has a bone through it, and how well you like it done – I like a medium steak. Remove the steaks from the pan, place on a plate, cover the steaks loosely with foil and allow to rest for 5 minutes.

6. Stir the aged balsamic into the tomatoes.

7. Dress a large board with the rocket leaves.

8. Place both rested steaks on the board and slice each steak into 1.5cm-thick strips at an angle. Spoon over the balsamic tomatoes, sprinkle over the remaining sauce from the pan and add a generous grating of fresh Pecorino or Parmigiano (if using).

9. Use the rosemary-infused extra virgin olive oil to drizzle over the dish with a little extra salt.

CARMELA'S TIPS:
- Make sure the steaks are at room temperature and not fridge cold when you cook them.
- Retain the tomato vines and use them in a stock, soup or sauce for added flavour.

Strozzapreti Pasta with Octopus and Tomatoes, *Strozzapreti pasta, polpo e pomodori*

This opulent dish is full of memories for me. I am a little obsessed with the humble octopus. It has incredible features, from its eight sucker-covered legs to the way it is able to flawlessly dance through the ocean. The octopus is the pick of the ocean for me, and the way it tastes when cooked correctly is just outstanding. Here, I have chosen to pair the king of the ocean with my love of pasta – a match made in heaven. The polpo sauce could be also spooned onto warm polenta.

Serves: 4
Preparation time: 20 minutes
Cooking time: 1 hour

salt and freshly ground black pepper
rustic bread, to serve

For the octopus
pinch of salt
800g fresh octopus
2 bay leaves
5 parsley stems
5 pink peppercorns

For the sauce
4 tbsp extra virgin olive oil
1 small carrot, finely diced
1 celery stick, finely diced
1 shallot, finely chopped
2 garlic cloves, crushed
300g cherry tomatoes, halved
300g passata
50ml water
1 tbsp finely chopped celery leaves
dried chilli flakes, to taste (optional)
400g strozzapreti pasta, or an alternative of your choice
small bunch of parsley, finely chopped

1. Bring a large saucepan of water to the boil and season it with a pinch of salt when it reaches the boil.

2. 'Shock' the octopus three times in the boiling water – this helps tenderise it. Dip the octopus in the boiling water, hold it there for 20 seconds with tongs and remove, being careful not to scald yourself. Repeat this action three times, then immerse the entire octopus in the pan. Add the bay leaves, parsley stems and pink peppercorns, clamp on a lid and cook over a medium heat for 30–40 minutes until tender.

3. Meanwhile, heat the olive oil in a shallow, wide sauté pan over a medium heat, add the carrot, celery and shallot and cook for 15 minutes until softened but not coloured.

4. Add the garlic and stir, then tumble in the cherry tomatoes and cook for 5 minutes. Remove from the heat.

5. Once the octopus is cooked, remove it from the pan and drain, chop the tentacles into small bite-size pieces and add them to the tomato sauce. Add the passata to the pan along with a generous pinch each of salt and pepper and the celery leaves. If you like a little heat, sprinkle in a few dried chilli flakes. Stir and cook the sauce for a further 15 minutes.

6. Bring a large pan of water to the boil for the pasta. Once boiling, season well with salt and cook the strozzapreti according to the packet instructions, but for 3 minutes less, ensuring the pasta remains al dente.

7. Drain the pasta – retain a small mugful of pasta water – and toss it into the sauce. If needed, add a little of the pasta water, stir, check for seasoning and sprinkle in the chopped parsley.

8. Serve in warm bowls with a little rustic bread.

CARMELA'S TIP:
- If you are cooking fresh octopus within inland UK, you will need to pre-order it, so please ensure you allow time for this. Frozen octopus would suffice.

Stuffed Artichokes, *Carciofi ripieni*

I adore these straight from the jar and served as part of my antipasti, sliced on pizza, filled and deep-fried (see page 76) or steamed from fresh, as below. Artichokes are beautiful to look at, yet can be incredibly intimidating to the novice cooks among us – please do not allow the preparation to put you off, as this humble vegetable is worth your time. I remember, as a little girl, watching my aunty and uncle eat the artichokes, stripping the goodness from each leaf over their bottom teeth and sucking the leaves before throwing the empty leaves into a bowl in the centre of the dinner table. I used to think, *how strange, I will never do that!* How wrong was I?

Serves: 4
Preparation time: 30 minutes
Cooking time: 45 minutes– 1 hour

4 large artichokes
300g stale breadcrumbs
1 lemon, cut into wedges, and grated zest of ½ lemon
100ml extra virgin olive oil, plus 3 tbsp
2 plump garlic cloves, crushed
80g parsley leaves and stalks, finely chopped
salt and freshly ground black pepper

1. Cut off the stems of the artichokes and reserve.
2. Remove and peel away the firm outer leaves all the way around the artichokes. Using scissors, cut off the remaining sharp tips, then slice a couple of centimetres off the top of the artichokes. Open an artichoke a little, remove the fuzzy, inedible choke with a teaspoon, and discard. Repeat with the remaining artichokes. Wash them well and rub them with a fresh lemon wedge over all the raw, cut edges. Fill a bowl with water, squeeze in a little lemon juice, and place the artichokes in the bowl until you are ready to fill them. This will prevent them from discolouring.

3. Put the fresh breadcrumbs in a bowl along with the lemon zest, 100ml olive oil, a pinch each of salt and pepper, crushed garlic and chopped parsley. Stir well.
4. Remove the artichokes from the water and pat dry with kitchen paper. Leave them cut side down on kitchen paper for 5 minutes to remove any extra moisture. Fill the cavity of the artichokes with the breadcrumb mixture.
5. Fill a large pan with a 5cm-depth of water and add a pinch of salt and the 3 tablespoons of olive oil. Bring the water to a rolling boil. Roughly chop the stems and add them to the base of the pan, then add the artichokes to the pan so they stand vertically and are a snug, comfortable fit.
6. Cover with a lid and cook over a medium heat for 45 minutes–1 hour. The time they take to cook will vary depending on their size. Test with a knife to see if they are tender.
7. Remove from the pan and serve one artichoke per person, and enjoy as a starter.

CARMELA'S TIP:
*   Make extra!

Stuffed Sardines, *Sarde ripiene*

Some people may think cheese and fish do not necessarily marry well, but each to their own. (I whisper as I say this: I enjoy the combination!) Parmigiano-Reggiano adds a fantastic salty umami taste here as it mixes with the breadcrumbs and sits between these beautiful freshly filleted sardines. Only fresh sardines will do here, and ask your fishmonger to fillet them too, as they can be a little fiddly. The head will need to be removed and the backbone too, so that you can fill them and re-form them for baking.

Serves: 4
Preparation time: 25 minutes
Cooking time: 15 minutes
You will need: cocktail sticks

30g sultanas
750g sardines, scaled, gutted and butterflied
6 tbsp stale breadcrumbs
5 tbsp grated Parmigiano-Reggiano
2 garlic cloves, crushed
1 tbsp chopped parsley
1 tbsp finely chopped celery leaves
1 tbsp chopped fennel fronds
grated zest and juice of 1 lemon
4 tbsp olive oil, plus extra for drizzling
salt and freshly ground black pepper
fresh leaf salad, to serve

1. Preheat the oven to 190°C fan (410°F/gas 6).
2. Soak the sultanas in a bowl of warm water for 15 minutes.
3. Clean and open out the pre-filleted sardines.
4. Put the breadcrumbs, Parmigiano, garlic, parsley, celery leaves, fennel and drained sultanas in a bowl. Season with salt and pepper, add the lemon zest and mix to combine. Pour the olive oil into the breadcrumb mixture and stir.

5. Divide the mixture between each sardine and fill the cavities, then close and secure each sardine using a cocktail stick. Place the sardines in an ovenproof dish, drizzle over the remaining oil and spritz over the lemon juice.
6. Bake in the oven for 15 minutes, or until cooked through, then remove from the oven and serve the fish with a fresh leaf salad.

Sun-dried Tomatoes, *Pomodori secchi*

When you have a glut of tomatoes to enjoy, look ahead and prepare some sun-dried fare for your larder. They not only make a great addition to antipasti and light lunches, but are also lovely to snack on. Sun-drying tomatoes is an ancient way of preserving them: all that's required is ripe tomatoes, sunshine and dry weather. Sun-dried tomatoes are intense in flavour, so a little does go a long way. I prefer to use small plum tomatoes, however the best variety to use are 'Roma', as they have fewer seeds than most other varieties. This is the traditional method, so it does call for the sun, however you can also use a dehydrator or a low oven.

Makes: 2 x 200g jars/1 larger jar
Preparation time: 15 minutes
Drying time: 2–4 days

20 medium roma (plum) tomatoes
1 tbsp salt
2 garlic cloves, thinly sliced
1 tsp dried oregano or marjoram
extra virgin olive oil, for topping up the jars

1. Slice the tomatoes in half lengthways then place them cut side up on a wire rack and sprinkle lightly with salt.
2. Place the rack outside in direct sunlight and leave them out all day, remembering to bring them in again in the evening. Depending on the intensity of the sun, this process may take 2–4 days.
3. Once dried, place the tomatoes in a sterilised jar/jars along with slices of garlic in each jar and a sprinkle of the oregano or marjoram. Top up with extra virgin olive oil. Seal the jars.
4. The tomatoes will keep in the fridge or larder for up to 4 months. Once opened, keep in the fridge and consume within 2 weeks.

Oven-drying method
1. Preheat the oven to 80°C fan (150°F/gas 1).
2. Halve the tomatoes and place them cut side down on kitchen paper to remove excess moisture.
3. Sit the tomatoes on a wire rack – this will ensure the warm air circulates well – transfer to the oven, close the oven door and leave the tomatoes to dry for 6–8 hours.
4. Once the tomatoes have dried, remove from the oven and follow the process above, packing them into a jar/jars.

Dehydrator method
1. Turn on your dehydrator 20 minutes before it is required.
2. Halve the tomatoes and place them cut side down on to kitchen paper to remove excess moisture.
3. Sit the tomatoes on the plastic trays of the dehydrator, ensuring that they are well spaced to allow the air to circulate. Dehydrate for 8–12 hours, or according to the manufacturer's instructions.
4. Once the tomatoes have dried, follow the process above, packing them into a jar/jars.
   Please note that dehydrating times vary from one machine to another.

Veal rolled with Courgette Flowers and served with Tagliatelle,

vitello al ragù di fiori di zucchini e tagliatelle

Courgettes are a summer delight but, for me, their delicate sunbeam flowers have to be the highlight, don't you agree? Fragile as they may be, they are still incredibly versatile. Chopped into a seasonal frittata, filled and stuffed to their brim with ricotta and anchovy, dipped in batter and fried or tossed through pasta or risotto bianco. When I received a large haul from my parents' allotment I split them open, removed the stamen, rolled them into some veal escalopes and slowly cooked them. Serve the sauce with pasta and enjoy the braciola (the rolled and filled escalope) as a second course with salad and rustic bread.

Serves: 4
Preparation time: 30 minutes
Cooking time: 3 hours
You will need: cocktail sticks

8 veal escalopes
½ tsp dried oregano
8 courgette flowers, washed and internal buds removed
small bunch of basil
80g untoasted pine nuts, chopped
6 tbsp extra virgin olive oil
1 small carrot, finely diced
1 celery stick, finely diced
1 large shallot, finely diced
2 large garlic cloves, finely chopped
1 x 600g jar passata
400g tin of plum tomatoes
200ml water
1 tbsp tomato purée
Parmesan rind (optional)
350g fresh egg tagliatelle
100g Parmigiano-Reggiano, grated
salt and freshly ground black pepper

1. Lay the sliced veal on a sheet of baking parchment and top with another sheet. Take a meat tenderising mallet or rolling pin and gently pound the meat to flatten it out evenly, taking care not to tear or damage the veal.

2. Remove the baking parchment and season the flattened escalopes with salt, pepper and a sprinkle of the oregano.

3. Open out a courgette flower onto each escalope. Add a couple of basil leaves onto each escalope and sprinkle on a few chopped pine nuts, then roll each escalope and secure the rolls with cocktail sticks.

4. Heat 4 tablespoons of the extra virgin olive oil in a large saucepan over a low heat. Add four of the escalope rolls (braciole) and sear for 6 minutes, turning them with tongs until just coloured all over. Remove the braciole from the saucepan, set aside and repeat with the remaining braciole.

5. Heat the remaining oil in the same pan over a gentle heat, add the carrot, celery and shallot and fry for 10 minutes until softened and lightly coloured, then add the garlic, stir, and cook for 1 minute. Pour in the passata, plum tomatoes and water, stir and season with salt and pepper. Add the tomato purée, Parmigiano rind (if using) and the remaining basil and stir. Reintroduce the braciole to the pan and cook slowly over a low heat for 3 hours, uncovered. If the sauce becomes a little dry then add water as required.

6. Once the sauce is cooked and the braciole are tender, bring a large saucepan of water to the boil for the pasta. Once boiling, salt the water well and cook the pasta for 4 minutes or until al dente.

7. Remove the braciole from the pan and keep them warm.

8. Using tongs, add the tagliatelle to the sauce along with 40g of the grated Parmigiano and serve. Top with the remaining Parmigiano and place the braciole in the centre of the table.

CARMELA'S TIP:
- I also like to break up the braciole into the sauce and stir the veal through the tagliatelle pasta. Remove the Parmigiano rind before serving. This is the chef's perk!

Autumn

The view from my kitchen window changes – autumn arrives and with it the fall of the first autumnal leaves, creating an amber-golden carpet that, with dry, cold days, soon becomes crispy and dry beneath my feet. The crunch and aroma make me smile from ear to ear because, without fail, this is the season I long for every year. Wrap me up, keep me warm, feed me well. Autumn is a season where I bulk out a little, craving the warmth of comfort and the need to feel safe, with a plentiful kitchen around me.

Let chestnut and porcini soup, pan-fried polenta with gorgonzola and mushrooms, romanesco cauliflower fritters, polenta pizza, Barolo risotto and ribollita soup tease you into pulling on your wellies and join me in a chapter that will fill your tummy and your mind with ideas, recipes, tips and so much more.

As soon as a new season joins us in the UK, we should embrace its ingredients. For me, autumn is all about pumpkins and squashes – my pumpkin and amaretti tortellini and pumpkin risotto showcase this plump vegetable perfectly.

Potatoes, rice, polenta and pasta play an integral part in autumn and winter alike. They are the vessels to carry, fill and sustain us through the colder months in an inexpensive, simple but varied manner. Nothing to hide behind, only good, wholesome food.

Abruzzo Fish Stew, *Brodetto*

The UK coastline is so incredibly beautiful, but I couldn't live further inland if I tried. I'm based an hour away from London, in the county of Northamptonshire. Living inland means fresh fish has to be ordered in advance if you want to achieve a little rustic seafood perfection, so planning ahead is essential when I need to prepare and cook seafood for my family or my fortnightly supper club. I tend to order my fish in bulk and freeze it for ease and speed.

Serves: 6
Preparation time: 20 minutes
Cooking time: 40 minutes

1.5 litres fresh fish stock
170g mussels
200g clams
3 tbsp extra virgin olive oil
1 tsp fennel seeds
2 medium shallots, thinly sliced
1 celery stick, finely diced
1 small fennel bulb, quartered and thinly sliced
(retain and finely chop the fronds)
2 garlic cloves, crushed
1 small fresh red chilli, deseeded and finely chopped
8 San Marzano tomatoes (or good-quality plum tomatoes), roughly chopped
2 red mullet, scaled, gutted and filleted
1 small plaice, filleted
small bunch of parsley, stems and leaves separated and finely chopped
salt and freshly ground black pepper

1. Warm the fish stock in a saucepan over a low heat and season to taste. Simmer for 30 minutes until slightly reduced.
2. Clean and prepare the mussels and clams, carefully removing any large barnacles from the mussels and ensure the shells of the mussels and clams are all closed and unbroken. If any are damaged and open, discard. Wash them well and set aside until required.

3. Heat the oil in a large saucepan over a low heat, add the fennel seeds and gently toast for 3 minutes, watching them as you don't want them to catch or burn. Add the shallots, celery and fennel, increase the heat to medium and cook for 10 minutes until softened and translucent. Add the garlic, chilli and roughly chopped tomatoes and cook for 5 minutes.
4. Pour the reduced stock and chopped fennel fronds into the pan of tomatoes, then add the fish fillets and the parsley stems. Cook for 7 minutes and season to taste with salt and pepper.
5. Add the shellfish to the pan, clamp on a lid and cook for 5 minutes, shaking the pan intermittently until all the shells have opened fully. Taste and adjust seasoning accordingly.
6. Remove from the heat, sprinkle over the chopped parsley and serve with a ladle and an offering from a bread basket.

Barolo Risotto, *Risotto al Barolo*

A wonderful, simple risotto that is lifted with the richness of a full-bodied Barolo wine. I have decided to keep this risotto as simple as possible, as I want the carnaroli rice plump and the ruby warmth of the Barolo to shine through. If preferred, you can begin the risotto with a standard soffritto and even add some wonderful autumn mushrooms through the risotto for added texture. What is vital here is the quality of your stock. Homemade is preferable, however a good-quality deli stock or fresh supermarket stock would suffice.

Serves: 4
Preparation time: 10 minutes
Cooking time: 25 minutes, plus resting time

1.5 litres beef stock
60g salted butter
1 tbsp olive oil
1 large banana shallot, finely chopped
1 bay leaf
1 garlic clove, crushed
400g carnaroli risotto rice
250ml Barolo red wine
60g Parmigiano-Reggiano, grated, plus extra to serve
2 tbsp finely chopped parsley leaves and stalks

1. Warm the stock gently in a saucepan over a low heat. Taste the stock and check for additional seasoning.
2. Melt half the butter in a large, shallow sauté pan with the olive oil over a low heat, add the chopped shallot and cook for about 7 minutes, until softened and translucent. Add the bay leaf and crushed garlic, stir, and cook for a further 2 minutes. Sprinkle in the rice and stir with a wooden spoon to ensure that each grain is covered in the shallot juices, toasting it for 1 minute, then pour in the wine and stir and cook for 2 minutes until the wine has been absorbed.
3. Slowly begin to add the fish stock, one ladle at a time, stirring frequently for 20 minutes or so until the rice has absorbed the

stock. For a beautifully rich risotto, I urge you to stand and continuously stir the rice with a wooden spoon that has a hole in the centre (if you have one). Remove the bay leaf, taste and season as required.

4. Remove the risotto from the heat and add the remaining butter, the grated Parmigiano and the chopped parsley. Stir, cover the pan with a clean tea towel and clamp on a lid. This stage is called *la mantecatura* (see page 14) and it should never be missed. If your hunger allows, then I suggest allowing the risotto to rest for 5–10 minutes.

5. Spoon onto warmed plates and add an extra sprinkling of grated Parmigiano.

Beetroot and Ricotta Raviolo with Browned Butter and Sage Leaves,

Barbabietole e' ricotta raviolo con burro e salvia

I love beetroots, especially when I'm able to find the candy-striped ones that are delicately striped, rotund and brightly coloured. Bought fresh and roasted with a little olive oil, a pinch of salt, garlic cloves and a small bunch of lemon thyme, they are simply heavenly. They make for a great side dish, roasted and chopped through a risotto, or puréed and used as a pasta filling. A delicately piped circle of the beetroot and ricotta purée will house the egg yolk and make the most amazing raviolo you'll ever eat. This dish makes for a perfect starter.

Serves: 4
Preparation time: 1 hour, including 30 minutes resting time
Cooking time: 5 minutes
You will need: a pasta machine, a 9cm plain or fluted round pastry cutter, and a piping bag (optional)

200g semola flour, plus extra for dusting
200ml full-fat milk
400g fresh beetroot, peeled
extra virgin olive oil, for drizzling
300g ricotta
¼ tsp freshly grated nutmeg
80g Parmigiano-Reggiano, grated, plus extra to serve
4 egg yolks
90g salted butter
8 small sage leaves
salt and freshly ground black pepper

1. To make the dough, tip the flour onto a board or clean work surface, make a well in the centre and add the milk. Combine and knead until smooth. Cover with cling film and allow the dough to rest for 30 minutes at room temperature.
2. Preheat the oven to 180°C fan (400°F/gas 6).

3. Cut the beetroot into 1cm cubes and tumble it into an oven dish, drizzle with olive oil and season with salt and pepper. Stir well, cover with foil and roast for 30 minutes until tender.

4. Remove from the oven and allow the beetroot to cool for 15 minutes, then pop it into a food processor and blitz until smooth. Scrape the beetroot purée into a clean bowl and add the ricotta, then stir with a spatula to combine. Add the grated nutmeg and Parmigiano and season with salt and pepper, tasting and adjusting the flavour to suit your palate. Spoon the mixture into a small piping bag and place in the fridge until required. (Using a piping bag makes the filling easier to pipe.)

5. Uncover the pasta dough, cut it in half and dust it generously with semola (or '00' flour if preferred). Re-cover one half of the dough so that it doesn't dry out. Push the other half of the dough down using your palms to make a flat disc and pass it through the pasta machine on the widest setting. Envelope the dough (fold it in half), dust it with flour and repeat passing it through the machine six times on the widest setting, then pass the dough twice through sequentially thinner settings until you reach the penultimate setting, leaving you with a long, thin sheet of pasta. Repeat with the other half of the dough, then cut each sheet of pasta into eight 8 x 9cm discs using a plain or fluted round pastry cutter.

6. Pipe a circle of the beetroot filling onto 4 discs, leaving a small hole in the centre for the egg yolk and a 1cm gap around the outside so you are able to seal the ravioli securely. Delicately place a yolk into the centre of each circle of beetroot purée. Sprinkle a pinch of Maldon salt on top of each yolk for added seasoning.

7. Using a pastry brush or the tip of your index finger, run a little water around the outside of each ravioli disc. Top the base of the ravioli with a plain pasta disc and secure. Sit the ravioli on a little dusting of semola flour to prevent sticking.

8. Bring a large pan of water to the boil. Once boiling, salt it well.

9. Cook the ravioli for 3–4 minutes, until the edge of the raviolo is tender. The aim is to keep the yolk deliciously dippy.

10. Melt the butter in a shallow frying pan with a pinch of salt over a low heat and add the sage leaves. Cook gently until the butter has started to brown and the sage leaves have crisped up a little.

11. Using a slotted spoon remove the ravioli from the water and plate them up with a drizzle of browned butter, the sage leaves and a generous grating of Parmigiano.

CARMELA'S TIP:
- The beetroot filling can be made a day in advance to save time.

Bolognese Ragú, from The Accademia Italiana della Cucina, *Bolognese ragú*

The varieties and variations of a Bolognese ragù are truly endless. What I love more that anything is that every family, whether they be in the UK or happily living in one of the twenty regions of Italy, will have their own take on this much-loved and respected classic recipe. I have chosen to share with you one taken from The Accademia Italiana della Cucina, a cookery school in the city of Bologna.

Serves: 4
Preparation time: 15 minutes
Cooking time: 2 hours 45 minutes

150g pancetta, cut into small cubes
20g salted butter
1 tbsp extra virgin olive oil
50g carrot, finely chopped
50g celery, finely chopped
50g onion, finely chopped
300g coarsely minced beef
80ml glass red wine
300g tomato passata or 1 x 400g tin plum tomatoes
70ml full-fat milk
40ml double cream, to finish (optional)
400g tagliatelle
salt and freshly ground black pepper
50g Parmigiano, grated, to serve

1. Heat a dry saucepan over a low heat, add the pancetta and fry for 5 minutes until lightly coloured, then add the butter and olive oil along with the carrot, celery and onion. Cook for 15 minutes over a medium heat until softened and translucent.

2. Add the beef and cook for 10 minutes, breaking up the beef with a wooden spoon and letting it colour all over before pouring in the red wine. Allow the wine to evaporate. Stir and add the passata or tinned plum tomatoes (breaking up the tomatoes with the back of the wooden spoon). Season with salt and pepper and cook over a low heat for 2 hours, uncovered. Stir intermittently and check for additional seasoning.
3. After 2 hours, slowly stir in the milk and optional cream, adjust seasoning as required and cook for a further 30 minutes.
4. Just before serving, cook the tagliatelle in a large saucepan of boiling salted water until al dente. Drain and dress with the ragù.
5. Serve with a dusting of Parmigiano.

CARMELA'S TIP:
- As I mention above, this is the traditional recipe, however you could also add some fresh basil leaves to finish, and a little garlic in the soffritto base.

Cappellacci filled with Rabbit, Veal and Pork, *Cappellacci con coniglio*

Anyone who follows me on Instagram will know that this is my favourite filled pasta to make – I might even go so far as saying I am obsessed with this shape. This meat cappellacci is served with browned butter and a flurry of Parmigiano. I adore the filling and can happily eat it straight from the pan, so I always suggest making a little more than you need. Make the filling a day in advance, as it benefits no end from being chilled.

Serves: 4
Preparation time: 1 hour
Cooking time: 2 hours
You will need: a pasta machine, a 6cm fluted round pastry cutter

For the filling
30g unsalted butter
2 tbsp olive oil
1 celery stick, finely diced
1 carrot, finely diced
1 medium white onion, finely diced
2 garlic cloves, thinly sliced
300g boned rabbit meat, roughly chopped
200g loin of veal, cut into 1 cm cubes
100g boned pork shoulder, cut into small pieces
1 tbsp tomato purée
125ml red wine
800ml vegetable stock
250g spinach
70g Parmigiano-Reggiano, grated, plus extra to serve
¼ tsp freshly grated nutmeg
2 egg yolks
400g egg pasta dough (page 165)
semola, for dusting
salt and freshly ground black pepper

For the sauce
3 tbsp salted butter
50ml cooking juices
4 sage leaves

1. Heat the butter and olive oil in a large, shallow pan over a low heat. Tumble the celery, carrot, onion and garlic into the pan and cook for 10 minutes.
2. Add the rabbit, veal and pork, then stir and cook for about 10 minutes to sear the meat all over.
3. Add the tomato purée, red wine and vegetable stock, season with salt and pepper, cover and cook over a medium heat for 1 hour 30 minutes, checking it again near the end for seasoning and adjusting as necessary.
4. Meanwhile, blanch the spinach briefly in a pan of boiling water, then drain, squeeze out any excess water, chop finely and set aside.
5. Drain any juices from the meat and retain 50ml of them. Put all the remaining contents of the pan in a food processor and blitz gently until roughly minced. Add the chopped spinach, grated Parmigiano, nutmeg and egg yolks and blitz for 30 seconds. Stir, taste and check for seasoning, then spoon the filling mixture into a bowl, cover and chill. This could be made a day ahead to save time.
6. Roll the pasta dough out into long lasagne sheets with a pasta machine (see method in the Beetroot and Ricotta Raviolo recipe on page 121), finishing on the penultimate setting of your pasta machine. Cut the sheets of dough with a fluted round pastry cutter into 6cm circles.
7. Pinch pieces of the pre-made meat filling and roll into balls. Place a meaty ball onto the centre of each round pasta disc.
8. Take a pasta disc into your hand and fold it in half, forming a half moon. Holding the half moon (mezzaluna) in your hand with the curved surface facing upwards, simply press the two corners together, leaving you with a cheeky, bottom-like pasta shape.
9. Repeat as required until you have used all of your pasta dough and filling. This amount will make more than 40 cappellacci. Place the prepared pasta on a tray lightly dusted with semola.

10. Bring a large saucepan of water to the boil, then salt it well. Cook the cappellacci in the boiling water for about 4 minutes until cooked through and al dente.
11. To make the sauce, melt the butter in a sauté pan over a medium heat along with the sage leaves and add the 50ml of reserved cooking juices. Cook for 5 minutes.
12. Drain the cappellacci and place them in the sauce using a slotted spoon.
13. Spoon into warm bowls and scatter over extra Parmigiano.

CARMELA'S TIP:
• Please have a look at my Instagram account for advice and tips on shaping pasta, and for video tutorials #carmelaskitchen.

Chestnut and Porcini Soup,

Minestra di castagne e porcini

BANG! I would hear my mum utter a string of mild swear words under her breath because my dad Rocco had forgotten to cut a cross at the base of each chestnut before they were met with the heat of the Aga. A memory like this is a reassuring reminder – I never forget now – that the cross is vital. However, I do enjoy this soup out of season so, as mentioned below, vacuum-packed or tinned chestnuts make a quick and tasty alternative. If using fresh chestnuts, ensure you remember to soak them after shelling, the night before use.

Serves: 4
Preparation time: 10 minutes
Cooking time: 50 minutes

450g cooked and peeled whole chestnuts
80g salted butter
2 large banana shallots, thinly sliced
50ml full-fat milk
50ml single cream
500ml vegetable stock
2 tbsp extra virgin olive oil
200g fresh porcini mushrooms, thinly sliced
5 sprigs of thyme
salt and freshly ground black pepper

1. For fresh chestnuts, soak the chestnuts in bowl of water overnight, covered, at room temperature. Vacuum-packed chestnuts don't require soaking.
2. Melt the butter in a medium saucepan over a medium heat, add half the sliced shallots and fry gently for about 15 minutes until softened and beautifully translucent.
3. Add the prepared chestnuts to the shallots along with the milk, cream and stock, and stir. Cook for about 40 minutes (the cooking time will depend on the size of the chestnuts) until the chestnuts are perfectly soft.

4. In the meantime, heat the olive oil in a frying pan over a medium heat, add the remaining sliced shallots and fry for 5 minutes, then add the sliced porcini and half the thyme and fry for a further 5 minutes.
5. Transfer half of the soup to a jug and blend to a smooth purée with a stick blender (or use a food processor). Return the soup to the pan. Season to taste with salt and pepper.
6. Add the pan-fried shallot and porcini to the soup (discarding the thyme sprigs), along with the leaves stripped from the remaining thyme. Stir and serve in warm bowls.

CARMELA'S TIP:
- If fresh porcini aren't available, use 50g dried porcini instead. Soak the porcini in a bowl of hot water for 30 minutes. Remove and chop the rehydrated mushrooms. Drain the liquid through a piece of muslin to remove small gritty debris, and use this strained porcini stock in the soup for additional flavour.

Chestnut Gnocchi with Mushrooms and Taleggio, *Gnocchi di castagne e fungi*

Echoes from the mountains with an autumnal mushroom seasonal note. This rich and decadent dish encompasses everything that is comfort in one bowl. Use a combination of your favourite mushrooms here. To reduce the richness, you could add half stock and half cream, but to be honest, in for a penny, in for a pound.

Serves: 4
Preparation time: 30 minutes
Cooking time: 30 minutes

For the gnocchi
1kg King Edward potatoes
1 egg
200g chestnut flour
salt and freshly ground black pepper

For the sauce
50g dried porcini
1 tbsp olive oil
20g salted butter
1 shallot, thinly sliced
1 garlic clove, thinly sliced
300g mixed mushrooms, sliced
400ml double cream
150g Taleggio
leaves from a sprig of thyme

1. First, make the gnocchi. Boil the potatoes (skins on) in a saucepan of boiling salted water for about 25 minutes until tender (the cooking time will depend on the size of your potatoes). Drain, allow the potatoes to cool, then peel and rice the potatoes through a potato ricer into a large bowl. I prefer to use a potato ricer, as it ensures a lump-free mix, however a potato masher will also do the job.
2. Put the porcini in a small heatproof bowl and cover with boiling

water. Allow the mushrooms to rehydrate for 20 minutes, then drain and chop the porcini (reserving the water if you like – see Tip). Set aside.

3. Heat the olive oil and butter in a shallow sauté pan over a medium heat, add the shallot and cook for about 7 minutes until just softened and lightly coloured. Add the garlic and sliced mushrooms, stir and cook for about 10 minutes until lightly browned, then stir in the chopped porcini and cream. Add the Taleggio and, once it's melted, taste and season as required. Add the thyme leaves and cook for a further 10 minutes.

4. Crack the eggs into the bowl of potato, spoon in the chestnut flour and season with salt and pepper. Form into a dough, being careful not to over-knead the dough (which will make the gnocchi tough).

5. Divide the dough into four portions and roll each portion into a long sausage with a thickness of about 2cm, then cut each sausage into 3cm-long pieces. Roll the gnocchi down the prongs of a fork or use a wooden gnocchi board, sushi mat or ribbed butter pat to create ridges, to make the gnocchi rigate.

6. Bring a large 5-litre saucepan of water to the boil, salt it and add all the gnocchi. When they bop to the top (after about 3 minutes' cooking time), cook them for a further 2 minutes.

7. Drain and tumble the gnocchi into the sauce.

8. Serve the gnocchi and sauce in warm bowls and fall in love with the comfort food of autumn.

CARMELA'S TIP:

*   Strain the porcini liquid through a fine sieve and make pasta with it. A combination of porcini water and semolina would make a wonderful *semola cavatelli*. Also, if the sauce needs to be loosened a little, feel free to use the cooking water from the gnocchi.

Chicken and Rice from Lombardy,

Riso alla pitocca

This is such a great dish to make as a Monday evening dinner, using the leftover chicken from your Sunday roast. Whenever I have roast chicken, I always cook two, aiming to have some leftovers for this recipe in my fridge. However, I find myself pinching mouthfuls of it and eating it straight from the fridge, topping it with a little salt. Leftovers in my house are few and far between, thanks to a large family with an even larger appetite.

Serves: 4
Preparation time: 10 minutes
Cooking time: 30 minutes, plus resting time

750ml homemade chicken stock (or an excellent quality liquid stock)
2 tbsp extra virgin olive oil
1 large shallot, finely chopped
2 garlic cloves, crushed
600g cooked chicken (leg and breast meat), chopped into bite-sized pieces
280g carnaroli risotto rice
150ml dry white wine or vermouth
1 bay leaf
30g salted butter
70g Grana Padano, grated, plus extra to serve
2 tbsp finely chopped celery leaves
1 tbsp finely chopped parsley

1. Warm the stock in a saucepan and taste for additional seasoning.
2. Heat the oil in a sauté pan over a medium heat, add the shallot and garlic and fry for 5 minutes until soft and translucent. Add the chopped chicken and cook for 10 minutes, then add the risotto rice and toast it, stirring, for 2 minutes. Now pour in the white wine or vermouth, stir again and allow the wine to evaporate.
3. Pour all of the stock in the pan and add the bay leaf and a little salt and pepper. Cook over a medium heat for 18 minutes until the rice is al dente, stirring with a wooden spoon that has a hole

in the centre (if you have one) to ensure the rice doesn't catch on the base of the pan.

4. Once cooked, stir and remove from the heat. Discard the bay leaf.
5. Add the butter, Grana Padano, celery leaves and parsley and stir well. Cover the pan with a clean tea towel and clamp on a lid. Leave the risotto to rest for 5–10 minutes, then adjust seasoning to taste.
6. Serve on warm plates with an additional sprinkle of Grana Padano.

CARMELA'S TIP:

- Try to use plump free-range or organic chicken as the dish will always benefit from good-quality meat. To make your own chicken stock, put the carcass of the bird in a pan of water along with a bay leaf, chopped celery stick, carrot, shallot, 3 plum tomatoes and 2 unpeeled garlic cloves. Simmer for 1 hour and 30 minutes, strain through a sieve and season as required.

Mussels with Saffron, *Cozze allo zafferano*

I love this dish for its speed, plumpness, freshness and because the sauce that sits in each shell as well as in the base of the bowl is simply scrumptious. Abruzzo, the region where this dish hails from, benefits from both the Adriatic Sea as well as the cooler inland mountains, with the two incredibly different terrains creating diverse menus and styles of cooking. So, here are mussels in bianco (white sauce) with the golden amber hue of L'Aquila saffron from Abruzzo.

Serves: 4
Preparation time: 15 minutes
Cooking time: 15 minutes

600g mussels
4 tbsp extra virgin olive oil
2 shallots, finely chopped
2 garlic cloves, crushed
1g saffron steeped in 2 tbsp warm water
1 bay leaf
small bunch of parsley, finely chopped
125ml white wine or dry vermouth
salt and freshly ground black pepper
rustic bread, to serve

1. Clean and prepare the mussels, carefully removing any large barnacles and ensuring the mussel shells are all closed and unbroken. If any are damaged and open, simply discard. Wash them well and set aside until required.
2. Heat the oil in a large, shallow saucepan over a medium heat, add the shallots and fry for 10 minutes until softened, then stir in the garlic and saffron with its soaking water. Cook for 2 minutes.
3. Tumble in the mussels with the bay leaf, half of the chopped parsley and a pinch each of salt and pepper. Stir well, then pour in the wine or vermouth and stir again.
4. Clamp on the lid and cook for about 6 minutes until all the mussels have full opened, shaking the pan intermittently.
5. When cooked, stir and discard any mussels that are still closed.

6. Serve in a large warmed serving bowl, ladling over any sauce and sprinkling over the remaining chopped parsley, alongside a glass of something nice and a basket of rustic bread.

Pan-fried Polenta with Gorgonzola and Mushrooms, *Polenta al gorgonzola e funghi*

Indulgence will wait for no woman or man! This rich, decadent autumnal dish, using gorgonzola (from the region of Lazio) offers instant fulfilment. It's paired perfectly with pan-fried polenta, however the sauce would work equally well blanketing fresh gnocchi or spooned and drizzled over pasta.

Serves: 4–6
Preparation time: 20 minutes
Chilling time: 1 hour 30 minutes
Cooking time: 30 minutes
You will need: a 28 x 32cm baking tray

1 litre vegetable stock
250g quick-cook polenta, plus extra for dusting
150g salted butter, cubed
130g Parmigiano-Reggiano, grated
leaves from a sprig of thyme
1 banana shallot, thinly sliced
200g mixed mushrooms, thinly sliced
800ml double cream
300g gorgonzola
small bunch of parsley, finely chopped
100ml olive oil, plus 1 tbsp for frying
salt and freshly ground black pepper

1. Line the baking tray with baking parchment.
2. Bring the stock to a simmer in a saucepan over a medium heat.
3. Slowly and steadily add the polenta, whisking constantly with a firm whisk for 2 minutes, to prevent lumps forming. Once all the polenta has been added and the mixture is smooth, change to using a wooden spoon and beat the mixture for a further 7 minutes. Ensure the polenta doesn't catch on the bottom of the pan.
4. Once cooked, remove the pan from the heat and add 110g of the cubed butter and all the Parmigiano. Stir, taste for additional seasoning and add the thyme leaves.

5. Pour the polenta into the lined tray and leave at room temperature for 30 minutes, then place the tray in the fridge for at least 1 hour until it has set firm.
6. While the polenta is in the fridge, make the sauce. Heat the olive oil and remaining butter in a shallow sauté pan over a low heat, add the shallot and sliced mushrooms and fry for 10 minutes, then add the cream and heat until it reaches a simmer. Tumble in the gorgonzola and heat until melted. Season with a little salt and pepper to taste.
7. Remove from the heat, stir and add the chopped parsley. Check for additional seasoning.
8. Cut the set polenta into 4 x 8cm pieces. Heat the tablespoon of oil in a frying pan over a medium heat. Dip each piece in a little more polenta and fry it in the pan for 6 minutes or until lightly golden on both sides.
9. Serve the polenta in a stack and pour over a little of the creamy sauce.

CARMELA'S TIP:
- For a milder and slightly sweeter note, you could substitute the gorgonzola for dolcelatte and even add some chopped walnuts at the end, for texture and crunch.

Polenta

If I excitedly mutter the word 'polenta' the response I normally receive is a grunt of utter disappointment and dread. This makes me desperately sad because polenta is not only filling and inexpensive, it's warming, flavoursome and just perfect for this time of year. The key to polenta is to season it well, and literally pump it with masses of flavour. At home, my children call it Italian mash – for them they know no different at all.

Polenta is always a winner because of how I choose to make it and almost whip it. There are two types of polenta: the slow-cooked variety (bramata) which takes about 45 minutes and is superior, if time allows; and then there's the quick-cook variety, which takes roughly 8 minutes. (See notes in Introduction on page 15.)

Polenta is so incredibly versatile. The grain's uses range from making delicious polenta cake (see my first cookbook, *Southern Italian Family Cooking*), or mixing the grain with breadcrumbs to coat chicken pieces or fish before frying, to making my soft, whipped milk polenta, which is silky in texture with a reassuring smooth mellow taste. As well as adding lots of flavour, it's crucial to use a whisk when stirring (rather than a wooden spoon) because you need to eradicate any chance of gritty lumps forming.

Whipped Milk Polenta

Serves: 8
Preparation time: 5 minutes
Cooking time: 10 minutes

1 litre vegetable or chicken stock
500ml full-fat milk
380g quick-cook polenta
50g salted butter
100g Parmigiano-Reggiano, grated
1 tsp chopped parsley leaves
1 tsp chopped celery leaves
salt and freshly ground black pepper

1. Start by warming up the milk and chosen stock in a saucepan and bringing it to a rolling boil.
2. Very slowly pour in the polenta, whisking constantly with a firm whisk (otherwise lumps will form).
3. Cook, stirring with your whisk for 6–8 minutes over a medium heat, but be careful as the polenta has a tendency to spit. The polenta will gradually thicken – you are looking for a loose mash consistency.
4. Taste and season well, take the polenta off the heat and add the butter, grated Parmigiano and fresh chopped herbs. Stir well and serve immediately.

Polenta and Taleggio Fritters,

Frittelle di polenta e Taleggio

Polenta and Taleggio fritters are great for days when you have cooked polenta lurking in the fridge. The fritters freeze very well once fried, so this makes a perfect make-ahead recipe.

Serves: 4 as a starter
Preparation time: 15 minutes
Cooking time: 15 minutes (depending on the quantity and size)

3 medium floury potatoes, peeled and cut into 4cm chunks
250g leftover polenta
90g Taleggio, chopped
50g Grana Padano, grated
1 egg yolk
pinch of freshly grated nutmeg
3 tbsp light olive oil, plus extra if necessary
salt and freshly ground black pepper
Tomato Sugo (page 44), to serve (optional)

1. Bring a pan of water to the boil, salt it, then add the potatoes and cook until tender. Drain.
2. Put the leftover polenta in a large bowl and break it up, first using a potato masher, then using your hands to crumble the polenta.
3. Add the warm boiled potatoes to the polenta along with the chopped Taleggio, grated Grana Padano, egg yolk and nutmeg. Season with salt and pepper and mix well.
4. Heat the olive oil in a shallow frying pan over a medium heat. Form the mixture into small, palm-sized fritters and fry them evenly on both sides, in batches, for about 6 minutes until golden brown, turning them halfway through. Continue until all of the mixture has been used up.
5. Serve the fritters as a warm snack, or cold with a spoonful of fresh tomato sugo.

CARMELA'S TIP:
- Retain the egg white to add to a frittata.

Polenta Pizza, *Pizza di polenta*

Polenta, a grain that hails from the north of Italy and embodies the simple values of southern Italian *cucina povera* kitchens, is always a welcome treat, however I tend to find the UK palate struggles with this simple gluten-free grain, as it really requires masses of seasoning – something that some people are still wary of. Use a good-quality stock, not solely water, to make the polenta, remembering to finish it with a little butter, fresh herbs and lots of grated Parmigiano. This pizza base needs to be a little firmer than normal as you need to make, chill, bake and slice it as required.

Serves: 4
Preparation time: 10 minutes
Cooking time: 15 minutes

800ml vegetable or chicken stock (or milk)
200g quick-cook polenta
1 tsp dried marjoram or oregano
25g salted butter
80g Parmigiano-Reggiano, grated
pizza sauce (your choice), to taste
250g mozzarella, roughly torn
salt and freshly ground black pepper

To serve
basil leaves
rocket salad with a drizzle of balsamic vinegar

1. Preheat the oven to 190°C fan (410°F/gas 6) and line two baking trays with baking parchment.
2. Warm the stock or milk in a large, saucepan until it reaches a rolling boil.
3. Gently and gradually whisk in the polenta and continue to whisk as this will disperse any lumps for about 8 minutes over a medium heat until you have cooked out the grains (if whisking is too labour intensive, beat it with a wooden spoon with a hole in the centre). Season with salt and pepper.

4. Remove from the heat and add the butter and 50g of the grated Parmigiano. Stir and taste for additional seasoning.
5. Transfer the polenta to the lined trays with a spatula to make four round discs about 20cm in diameter (about size of a small dinner plate). Spoon on some pizza sauce, sprinkle over a little torn mozzarella, and bake in the oven for 15 minutes until it has lightly caught some colour.
6. Remove from the oven, sprinkle over the rest of the Parmigiano and some fresh basil, then slice and enjoy with a rocket salad and a drizzle of balsamic.

CARMELA'S TIP:
- Replace some of the liquid in the above recipe with the water from the bag of fresh mozzarella for added flavour.

Prune-stuffed Gnocchi, *Gnocchi di prugne*

These dried-fruit-filled gnocchi are a source of intrigue any time you mention them, as the ingredients are not characteristically Italian. The region of Friuli-Venezia Giulia is proud of its diversity and takes inspiration in its recipes from the surrounding countries that border the region, such as Austria and Slovenia.

Serves: 4
Preparation time: 30 minutes
Cooking time: 20–25 minutes
You will need: a potato ricer

1kg King Edward potatoes, washed (but not peeled)
30g salted butter, at room temperature
70g Parmigiano-Reggiano, grated
1 egg
280g '00' flour
230g stoned prunes, halved
80g salted butter
6 tbsp stale breadcrumbs
½ tsp ground cinnamon
salt and freshly ground black pepper

1. Bring a large pan of water to the boil and salt it well. Put the unpeeled potatoes in the pan and boil for 20–25 minutes until tender.
2. Drain the potatoes and allow them to cool until you are able to handle them easily.
3. Peel the potatoes, rice them with a potato ricer (or regular potato masher) and place them in a large bowl. Add the butter, grated Parmigiano and egg, mix to combine, then add the flour to the potatoes and season with a little salt and pepper. Stir the flour into the potatoes to form a ball of dough (don't work the mixture for longer than 1 minute as it will become glutinous and dense).

4. Divide the dough into four portions and roll each portion into long sausages about 2cm thick. Cut each sausage into 3cm-long pieces. Flatten the gnocchi into your palm, add the prune half, form in a ball and repeat with the remaining dough.
5. Bring a large 5-litre saucepan of water to the boil, salt it, then add the gnocchi. When the gnocchi bounce to the top (after about 3 minutes' cooking time), stir gently and cook for a further 3 minutes.
6. Melt the butter in a small pan until just browned.
7. Mix the breadcrumbs in a bowl with the cinnamon.
8. Drain the gnocchi and serve with the melted butter and a scattering of the cinnamon breadcrumbs.

Mantova-style Pumpkin and Amaretti Tortelli, *Tortelli di zucca e amaretti*

I decided to include this recipe from my second book, *A Passion for Pasta*, because of its regional connection, but really (and more simply) because it is one of my most memorable and loved pasta dishes I have had the pleasure of eating, cooking and developing. The sweetness of pumpkin paired with *mostardo di fruta* (mustard fruit) and crushed amaretti... words struggle to describe the absolute brilliance and sophistication of this plate of food. Get ready to taste what I consider to be one of the best pasta dishes, a dish that created my love and adoration for pasta.

Serves: 4
Preparation time: 30 minutes, plus 1 hour cooling time
Cooking time: 40 minutes
You will need: a pasta machine

400g egg pasta dough (page 165)
semola flour, for dusting
70g Grana Padano, grated, plus extra to serve
30g hard amaretti biscuits, crushed (optional)
salt and freshly ground black pepper

For the filling
1kg pumpkin, unpeeled, deseeded and cut into wedges
90g hard amaretti biscuits, crushed, plus extra to serve
150g Grana Padano, grated
100g mostarda di frutta, finely chopped
½ tsp freshly grated nutmeg
grated zest of 1 small lemon

For the sauce
1 tbsp olive oil
90g unsalted butter
15 sage leaves

1. Preheat the oven to 180°C fan (400°F/gas 6).
2. Roast the pumpkin wedges in a tray in the oven for 30 minutes, or until tender.
3. Remove from the oven and push the cooked pumpkin through a sieve into a bowl. Allow the smooth pulp to cool for 1 hour.
4. Add the crushed amaretti biscuits, grated Grana Padano, mostarda di frutta, nutmeg, and lemon zest to the pumpkin pulp, stir, taste and season with salt and pepper. Cover the mixture and set aside.
5. Roll out the pasta dough into sheets with a rolling pin, a broom handle or wine bottle, or using your pasta machine, which should be sitting proudly on your kitchen surface (follow the Beetroot and Ricotta Raviolo instructions on page 121). Place the pasta sheets on a surface lightly dusted with semola flour then cut them into squares measuring about 4 x 4cm.
6. Place a teaspoon of the filling mixture onto each pasta square. Using a little water on your fingers, dampen the corners of dough and fold each square to form a triangle, gently squeezing out any air. Hold the triangle with the point facing upwards, then join each of the lower two corners together forming a perfect – or for me, slightly wobbly – tortello. Repeat with the remaining dough and filling.
7. Bring a large 5-litre saucepan of water to the boil. Once boiling, salt it well, add the tortello and cook for 4 minutes until al dente.
8. Heat the oil in a frying pan over a low heat, then add the butter along with the sage leaves. Brown the butter for 3 minutes. Season with a pinch of salt.
9. Drain the pasta with a slotted spoon and transfer to warmed bowls. Add a delicate drizzle of the browned butter, then a final sprinkle of Grana Padano. I also love to add an extra crumble of amaretti biscuits to finish the dish.

Comforting Potatoes and Fontina,
Tartiflette alla Fontina

A change of season brings with it a change of temperature and weather. It's raining so hard outside and I can barely see through my kitchen window, so I've decided to stay put today – I will not be leaving the warmth of my house. I crave the comfort of carbs with the mellow yet pungent hint of cheese. There's only one dish to make: *Tartiflette alla Fontina*. The core ingredients are satisfying on their own, but pairing them with melted fontina – a semi-hard cow's cheese from the Aosta Valley – elevates this dish to another level.

Serves: 2–3
Preparation time: 10 minutes
Cooking time: 30 minutes

4 medium potatoes, peeled and cubed
25g salted butter
2 banana shallots, thinly sliced
150g pancetta, cubed (I prefer smoked)
4 fresh sage leaves
50ml vegetable stock
150g fontina, roughy sliced
salt and freshly ground black pepper
rustic bread, to serve (optional)

1. Boil the potatoes in a saucepan of salted water until just tender.
2. Preheat the oven to 180°C fan (400°F/gas 6).
3. Melt the butter in a medium frying pan over a medium heat, add the shallots, pancetta and sage and fry for 10 minutes until lightly golden in colour.
4. Drain the potatoes and roughly pat them dry with kitchen paper. Lay the cooked potatoes in the base of a medium oven dish.
5. Scrape in the shallots, sage and pancetta from the pan and add the vegetable stock.

6. Sprinkle over a little salt and pepper and stir. Top with the fontina slices and bake in the oven, uncovered, for 20 minutes until bubbling.
7. Serve as a side or with rustic bread.

Pumpkin Risotto with an Amaretto Crumb, *Risotto di zucca e' amaretti*

Risotto hails from the northern regions of Italy, where there are a few different types of this versatile rice grain. Arborio rice is the most popular risotto rice in the UK, followed by carnaroli. It is vital that risotto rice is used in this recipe, as each grain becomes voluptuous and the end results are simply sublime. Pour yourself a glass of wine and stir the risotto slowly. Your tool of choice should be a wooden spoon with a hole in the centre. This hole will aid in a creamy finale as you stir, as it helps release the rice's natural starch. Finish with Parmigiano and butter.

Serves: 4
Preparation time: 10 minutes
Cooking time: 1 hour 30 minutes, plus resting time

For the risotto
1.5 litres vegetable stock
4 tbsp olive oil
2 banana shallots, finely chopped
1 garlic clove, crushed
500g carnaroli risotto rice
200ml white wine or white vermouth
small bunch of parsley, finely chopped (including stems)
2 tbsp chopped celery leaves
50g salted butter
100g Parmigiano-Reggiano, grated, plus extra to serve
50g hard amaretti biscuits, broken into uneven crumbs
salt and freshly ground black pepper

For the pumpkin purée
small pumpkin or squash, halved and deseeded
extra virgin olive oil, for drizzling
300ml double cream
½ tsp freshly grated nutmeg

1. Preheat the oven to 190°C fan (410°F/gas 6) and line a baking tray with baking parchment.
2. First, make the pumpkin purée. Halve the pumpkin and remove all the seeds. Spread the seeds out on an unlined baking tray and sprinkle them with salt. Roast in the oven for about 15 minutes, until just coloured, then remove and leave to cool. The pumpkin seeds make a tasty snack.
3. Slice the pumpkin flesh into 4cm-thick slices and place the slices on the parchment-lined baking tray. Sprinkle with a little salt, drizzle over some olive oil and roast in the oven for about 40 minutes, until tender.
4. Remove from the oven and peel away and discard the skin. Place the pumpkin in a food processor and blitz for 30 seconds. Add the double cream, freshly grated nutmeg and a generous pinch each of salt and pepper and blitz until incorporated.
5. Put a few tablespoons of the pumpkin mixture at a time in a mouli or sieve placed over a bowl and push through, or turn with a spatula, to separate any fibres from the pumpkin flesh: this will leave you with the most wonderful, silky purée. Taste for additional seasoning, cover and set aside until required.
6. Warm the vegetable stock in a saucepan, taste and adjust the seasoning as required.
7. Heat the olive oil in a large saucepan over a low heat, tumble in the chopped shallots and garlic and cook for 5 minutes, then add the rice and stir, toasting it in the oil for 1 minute, before pouring in the white wine or vermouth. Cook until the wine has been absorbed, then sprinkle in half of the parsley.
8. Add the stock to the pan, a ladle at a time, stirring frequently with a wooden spoon that has a hole in the centre (if you have one). Once the rice has absorbed a ladle of stock, simply add another.
9. Cook the risotto for about 15 minutes, and before you've added all the stock add the pumpkin purée. Stir and allow the risotto to absorb the purée liquid. Continue to add stock until the risotto rice is cooked but still has a delicate al dente bite. Season to taste with salt and pepper then scatter in the remaining parsley and celery leaves.

10. Add the butter and Parmigiano and stir well. Cover the pan with a clean tea towel and clamp on a lid. Leave the risotto to rest for 5–10 minutes.
11. Ladle the risotto onto warm plates, tapping the bottom of the plate on the surface so the risotto falls beautifully into a single layer. Scatter over the crumbled amaretti biscotti and serve with additional Parmigiano.

CARMELA'S TIP:

- I like to use a Crown Prince squash. The squash provides such a wonderful amber colour with a silky, smooth texture.

Rolled, Filled and Baked Aubergine,
Involtini di melanzane

This vegetable is the foundation of so many incredible dishes, yet in the UK aubergine is still not loved and eaten as much as it is in Italy. Its bountiful figure is perfect for filling and baking: it makes the best pasta filling, and caponata from Sicily is a delight, as is layered parmigiana, to name just two variations that are loved and enjoyed over all regions in Italy. *Involtini* are filled sheets of aubergine that are then rolled and baked. This is a speedy and delicious dish.

Serves: 4
Preparation time: 30 minutes
Cooking time: 55 minutes
You will need: a 20 x 30cm oven dish

3 tbsp extra virgin olive oil
1 medium shallot, finely chopped
1 garlic clove, crushed
400g tin pelati (plum) tomatoes
50ml water
large bunch of basil
1 tbsp finely chopped celery leaves
4 tbsp '00' flour, seasoned with salt and pepper
2 eggs
2 aubergines, sliced lengthways to about the thickness of a 50-pence coin
light olive oil, for frying
100g Parmigiano-Reggiano or Pecorino Romano, grated
(retain a little for the topping)
400g mozzarella, drained, sliced and cubed (retain a little for the topping)
salt and freshly ground black pepper

1. Heat the extra virgin olive oil in a small saucepan over a medium heat, add the shallot and fry gently for about 5 minutes, until translucent. Add the crushed garlic, and cook for 2 minutes then add the tinned tomatoes and water to the pan (see Tip), and season with salt and pepper. Add 8 basil leaves and the chopped celery leaves and simmer for 30 minutes, crushing the plum

tomatoes with the back of a wooden spoon.

2. Meanwhile, put the flour in one shallow bowl and crack and beat the eggs in another. Season the eggs with salt and pepper.

3. Pour light olive oil into a frying pan to a depth of 2cm and place over a medium heat. Once it's hot, dip each aubergine slice in the flour, then into the egg, then gently lay the aubergine into the hot oil. Fry for 3 minutes on each side.

4. Repeat with all the aubergine slices. Once fried, remove from the pan and allow the slices to rest on kitchen paper to remove excess oil.

5. Preheat the oven to 180°C fan (400°F/gas 6).

6. Add a ladle of the tomato sauce to the oven dish, covering the base. Lay out the aubergine slices on a board or clean work surface. Season them with a little salt and pepper and sprinkle a little Parmigiano over each slice, along with some chopped mozzarella and a few basil leaves.

7. Roll each aubergine slice into a cylinder, then lay each pre-rolled aubergine lengthways into the ovenproof dish.

8. Spoon over the tomato sauce, along with a little more torn or cubed mozzarella and grated Parmigiano, and bake in the oven for 25 minutes, until bubbling and slightly burnished. Remove from the oven and serve.

CARMELA'S TIPS:

- I usually slice and salt my aubergine slices prior to using them, to remove excess water and any bitterness. This isn't required with this recipe, however if you prefer to salt then please do remember to remove most of the salt and squeeze out any excess moisture before frying them.
- I like to add mozzarella water (from the bag of the fresh mozzarella) to the sauce instead of or alongside a reduced amount of water.

Roman-style Tripe, *Trippa alla romana*

Love it or hate it, I have to include at least one tripe recipe in this book. I pondered over it for some time, as I can't bear the stuff. I have haunting memories from my childhood and can still smell the deep aroma whoofing from the kitchen. As I write this, I find myself pinching my nose! But, soak it in milk for 24 hours, wash it, slice it, coat it in breadcrumbs and deep-fry it and you have my attention – for a while at least. However, it's not about what I like, so I have chosen to showcase tripe classically cooked *alla romana*, paired with tomatoes and offered with a basket of rustic bread and a glass of red wine.

Serves: 4
Soaking time: 24 hours
Preparation time: 20 minutes
Cooking time: 2 hours

500g tripe, washed
500ml full-fat milk
1 tbsp white wine vinegar
3 tbsp extra virgin olive oil
2 shallots, thinly sliced
1 garlic clove, crushed
1 bay leaf
6 large tomatoes, peeled (see Tip)
6 mint leaves
60g Pecorino Romano, grated, plus the rind
salt and freshly ground black pepper

1. Place the tripe in a large bowl, cover with milk and leave to steep in the fridge for 12 hours or overnight.
2. After 12 hours, discard the milk and clean the tripe again. Place it back in the bowl, top with water and add the white vinegar. Leave it for a further 12 hours, covered, in the fridge.
3. Drain and wash the tripe.
4. Bring a large saucepan of water to the boil, add the tripe and boil for 1 hour.

5. Drain and slice the tripe into 2cm-thick strips.
6. Heat the oil in a medium saucepan over a medium heat, add the shallots and fry for about 10 minutes until softened and translucent. Stir and add the garlic, along with the bay leaf, then add the sliced tripe along with the peeled and chopped tomatoes and Pecorino rind. Season with a little salt and pepper and cook for 1 hour 30 minutes, until tender.
7. Remove from the heat and discard the bay leaf. Chop the mint leaves and add them to the pan.
8. Taste and adjust seasoning as required. Remove and discard the Pecorino rind and serve in warm bowls with a little Pecorino.

CARMELA'S TIP:

- To peel fresh tomatoes, cut a cross into the top of each tomato to break the skin and place the tomatoes in a heatproof bowl of just-boiled water. Leave them for 5 minutes, then drain. Once they are cool enough to hold, peel away the skin from the top of the cross and discard.

Romanesco Fritters, *Romanesco fritti*

This stunning brassica resembles a vivid green, tightly formed bouquet of flowers. Each floret is squeezed perfectly into the next. Broccolo romanesco is from the same family as the cauliflower and broccoli, so these make a good alternative if you can't find romanesco. Equally, a combination of all three would work beautifully. Romanesco offers a light tender bite and is also great company for pasta.

Serves: 4 as a starter
Preparation time: 10 minutes
Cooking time: 15 minutes

90g '00' flour
1 tbsp extra virgin olive oil
70ml white wine or vermouth
grated zest of 1 lemon, lemon then cut into wedges to serve
500ml vegetable oil
500g Romanesco, separated into small florets
Maldon sea salt, for sprinkling
salt and freshly ground black pepper

1. First, make the batter. Tip the flour into a large bowl and season it with salt and pepper. Whisk in the olive oil and white wine or vermouth, then add the lemon zest.
2. Whisk to incorporate, cover and chill in the fridge for at least 30 minutes.
3. Heat the vegetable oil in a small deep-fat fryer (a small saucepan will suffice) to 170°C (340°F), or until a piece of bread dropped into the oil browns within 30 seconds.
4. Dip each floret in the batter, shake off any excess batter and fry in the hot oil for 3 minutes until lightly golden and cooked through. Remove with a slotted spoon and drain on kitchen paper to remove excess oil. Repeat until all the florets have been fried (you may need to fry the florets in batches).
5. Serve on a platter with the lemon wedges and an extra sprinkle of salt.

Solidea's Chickpea Soup, *Minestra di ceci*

I dedicate this dish to my mum, Solidea. She is known to eat Italian beans and chickpeas straight from the tin. I smile whenever I make this bean stew because I instantly think of her pulling back the ring pull from a tin and using her fork to gently encourage the chickpeas to sit proudly before letting them fall into her mouth. Simple and effortless, she would say. This dish is from Rome, but it really shines through with the simplistic *cucina povera* style that I will never tire of. This dish calls for dried chickpeas, but good-quality tinned chickpeas can be used instead.

Serves: 4
Preparation time: 10 minutes, plus overnight soaking
Cooking time: 1 hour

250g dried chickpeas (or a 400g tin, drained)
sprig of rosemary, bruised
1 bay leaf
3 tbsp extra virgin olive oil, plus extra for drizzling
1 large shallot, thinly sliced
2 garlic cloves, crushed
1 carrot, finely diced
1 celery stick, finely diced
90g Parma ham or speck, thinly sliced
400g tin of pelati (plum) tomatoes, crushed
1.5 litres vegetable or chicken stock
2 tbsp finely chopped celery leaves
125g baby spinach leaves
salt and freshly ground black pepper

To serve
slices of rustic Italian bread
50g Parmigiano-Reggiano, grated

1. Soak the chickpeas in a bowl of water overnight, with the sprig of bruised rosemary and bay leaf.

2. Heat the oil in a saucepan over a medium heat, add the shallot and soften for 5 minutes, then add the garlic along with the carrot, celery and Parma ham or speck and cook for 10 minutes.
3. Drain the chickpeas and discard the rosemary and bay leaf. Add the chickpeas to the pan, along with the crushed plum tomatoes, stock and celery leaves. Season well with salt and pepper and cook for 45 minutes, stirring intermittently until the stew thickens a little.
4. Just before serving, stir in and wilt the spinach. Place a slice of rustic Italian bread in the base of a bowl and add a ladle of the soup. Drizzle over a little olive oil and generous grating of Parmigiano.

CARMELA'S TIP:

- Instead of the chickpeas I also like to use borlotti beans and cannellini beans for a different texture. If using a tin of chickpeas, retain the aquafaba liquid and use it in your pasta dough: 100g semola plus 50ml aquafaba makes a single portion of pasta.

Spinach and Cream Gnocchi,

Gnocchi alla spinaci e panna

These gnocchi add a little touch of opulence and offer warmth and comfort, especially through the colder months. They are incredibly simple to make as well as inexpensive and speedy, but the key to getting them right is to ensure you really wring out the blanched spinach, to get it as dry as possible so the gnocchi are easy to shape. I have served them here with browned butter as we are in the north of Italy, but if no one is looking I'd also serve them with a simple shop-bought cherry tomato sugo.

Serves: 4 as a starter
Preparation time: 35 minutes, including 20 minutes resting time
Cooking time: 45 minutes

200g spinach leaves
150g salted butter
1 banana shallot, finely chopped
1 garlic clove, crushed
2 eggs
115ml double cream
210g '00' flour
¼ tsp freshly grated nutmeg
6 fresh sage leaves
60g Parmigiano-Reggiano, grated
2 tbsp finely chopped chives
salt and freshly ground black pepper

1. Wilt the spinach in a dry pan or in a microwave for 2 minutes. Allow to cool then squeeze well to remove any additional water and finely chop.
2. Heat 50g of the butter in a large frying pan over a medium heat, add the shallot and fry for 7 minutes until softened and translucent but not coloured. Add the garlic and stir, then remove from the heat and allow to cool.

3. Whisk the eggs and cream in a bowl. Slowly add the flour, whisking as you go. Stir, then season with salt, pepper and the grated nutmeg. Add the spinach, shallot and garlic and mix well. Allow the mixture to rest at room temperature for 20 minutes.

4. Bring a large saucepan of water to the boil then add a generous pinch of salt.

5. Form the gnocchi mixture into quenelles using two tablespoons.

6. Drop a batch of gnocchi quenelle into the boiling water (cook the gnocchi in two batches) and cook until they float to the surface, then simmer for a further 5–7 minutes, removing them with a slotted spoon when they're ready. Repeat with the remaining gnocchi mixture.

7. Melt the remaining butter in a shallow frying pan over a low heat, add the sage leaves and a pinch each of salt and pepper and cook for a few minutes until the butter is lightly browned.

8. Place the gnocchi on a large sharing platter and spoon over the melted butter and sage leaves. Sprinkle over the grated Parmigiano along with a light scattering of the chopped chives.

CARMELA'S TIP:

- If the gnocchi is too wet to form into quenelles, simply add a little more flour to the mixture. If it is too dry, add a little milk.

Tagliatelle with Truffle, *Tagliatelle al tartufo*

Truffles grated over pasta suits me better than the gesture of a gift of jewellery. Truffles are rich in aroma, with a price point to match, and rough and bulbous in texture. I remember going truffle hunting with Savini Tartufi in Tuscany. I have such fantastic memories of the wonderful guide, Luca, and his truffle dog Nico (who I believe has now retired). Nico found umpteen truffles then we went back to the restaurant and enjoyed a banquet of dishes all using the fresh autumnal funghi. I prefer to use fresh truffles if possible as I find truffle-infused oil to be a little strong and, dare I say it, a little unappealing, even for my palate.

Serves: 4
Preparation time: 5 minutes
Cooking time: 15 minutes

80g salted butter
3 tbsp dry white wine
pinch of freshly grated nutmeg
350g fresh tagliatelle
70g Parmigiano-Reggiano, grated
80g truffle
salt and freshly ground black pepper

1. Bring a large saucepan of water to the boil and when boiling, salt it well.
2. Melt the butter in a small saucepan over a low heat. Add the white wine and let it bubble and reduce for about 5 minutes.
3. Cook the pasta according to the cooking instructions, or for 4 minutes if fresh.
4. Season the white wine and butter with salt and pepper.
5. Drain the pasta and reserve a ladle of the cooking water. Place the tagliatelle back in the pan and pour over the melted butter. Stir, add the Parmigiano, stir again, and if required, add a little of the reserved pasta water.
6. Serve in warmed bowls or on a large sharing platter with thin shavings of truffle.

CARMELA'S TIPS:
- If you are making fresh tagliatelle, make it using 100g '00' flour plus 1 large egg per portion.

Winter

Hats, scarfs, gloves, earmuffs and winter boots on. Living in the UK means rain is inevitable, and all we think about is what can we eat next. I wonder why that is? Comfort, pleasure, gluttony? No and yes... we need a little more sustenance in the colder months, and we need pleasure, warmth and comfort.

Winter in my kitchen means slow-cooked sugos and ragús bubbling away, slow-cooked meat, and lots of sauces, soups and bread. So much bread! Bread for an Italian is a necessity *per fare la scarpetta*, 'to scrape the bowl'. It may as well be the eleventh commandment. If I can eat something between a piece of folded bread, then I certainly will. If a vegetable can be filled with bread, then I will season and fill it. It is pure comfort and inexpensive *cucina povera* cooking.

Fontina fondue, hunter's style rabbit, slow-cooked Roman oxtail, pasta with Umbrian sausage, boiled meats with mostarda di frutta, beef agnolotti with hazelnuts and stewed castelluccio lentils. Now, who's hungry? This chapter is rich, a little calorific, but reassuringly perfect in every way possible. I'm sure you will love everything mentioned within it. Keep warm, eat well and share your love of food with family and friends this season.

Beef Agnolotti with Hazelnuts and Sage Butter, *Agnolotti al manzo*

This is how the Piedmontese enjoy making and serving one of their regional ravioli dishes. Indulgence and opulence come to mind, so less is more here, but like any mealtime I prefer to make extra, because who doesn't like room-temperature pasta, right? I suggest making the filling a day ahead: this will help the flavours improve and the mixture to thicken, while saving you a little time.

Serves: 4–6
Preparation time: 1 hour
Cooking time: 2 hours 45 minutes – 3 hours 45 minutes
You will need: a food processor, a piping bag fitted with a round nozzle and a fluted pastry wheel

For the pasta dough
250g '00' flour
2 eggs, plus 1 egg yolk
50g semola, for dusting

For the filling
3 tbsp extra virgin olive oil
1 large shallot, finely chopped
1 celery stick, finely chopped
3 garlic cloves, crushed
600g braising beef, cut into small pieces
250ml red wine
2 x 400g tins of pelati (plum) tomatoes
1 bay leaf
1 egg yolk
2 tbsp chopped parsley
salt and freshly ground black pepper

For the sage and hazelnut butter
100g salted butter
10 sage leaves
50g blanched hazelnuts, roughly chopped

1. First, make the pasta: Put the flour, eggs and yolk in a food processor and pulse for 2 minutes. Sprinkle a wooden board or clean work surface with a light dusting of semola, then knead the dough until smooth. Cover with cling film and allow to rest at room temperature for 30 minutes.

2. While it's resting, get started on the filling (if you have not made it in advance). Heat the oil in a medium saucepan over a medium heat, add the shallot and celery and cook for 15 minutes until softened and translucent. Add the garlic and cook for 2 minutes, stirring.

3. Add the beef and let it brown for 8 minutes or so, then pour in the red wine and cook for about 10 minutes until it has more or less evaporated. Add the tinned tomatoes and stir, breaking up the tomatoes with the back of a wooden spoon, then add the bay leaf and season with salt and pepper. Cook over a medium heat, uncovered, for 2–3 hours until the meat is tender, checking and stirring it intermittently.

4. Taste, adjust the seasoning as required, and allow the mixture to cool (discarding the bay leaf).

5. Blitz the beef filling mixture in a food processor along with the egg yolk (for extra richness) and the parsley until roughly blended (it needs to be blended fine enough to be pipeable). Scrape into a clean bowl, cover and chill in the fridge until required.

6. Take the pasta dough and pat it down into a large, flat disc. Using your rolling pin, a broom handle or wine bottle, roll the pasta out into a sheet (*sfoglia*) that's so thin you can see through it.

7. Place the chilled filling into a piping bag and pipe 4cm-long sausages of the filling across the length of the pasta sheet, leaving a 3cm gap between each piece of filling.

8. Fold the pasta sheet over the filling and secure using a finger dampened with a little water to seal the pasta. Trim the edges and use a fluted pastry wheel to cut between each filled section, cutting yourself perfect agnolotti. Repeat until you have used all of the pasta and filling mixture.

9. Bring a large 5-litre pan of water to the boil. Once boiling, salt it well.

10. Melt the butter for the sauce in a frying pan over a low heat and add the sage and hazelnuts. Cook for about 5 minutes until the butter is lightly browned.
11. Cook the pasta for 4 minutes, until al dente.
12. Place the drained pasta on a warm platter and spoon over the browned butter and toasted hazelnuts.

Bread Dumplings with Speck and Salami, *Canederli di speck e salumi in brodo*

There are many variations of canederli across Italy. My variation of Southern Italian polpette are very similar, but they have the beauty of cured meat added to them. Canederli are popular in the Trentino area of Italy and are their version of plump gnocchi. Serve as here, in stock, or drizzle with melted butter and serve with lashings of grated Parmigiano.

Serves: 4
Preparation time: 40 minutes, including 30 minutes resting and soaking time
Cooking time: 40 minutes

600g stale breadcrumbs
250ml full-fat milk
100g thinly sliced speck
60g salami, roughly sliced
2 garlic cloves, crushed
2 tbsp finely chopped chives
4 eggs
80g Parmigiano-Reggiano, grated, plus extra to serve
2 tbsp '00' flour
1 litre beef stock
salt and freshly ground black pepper

1. Place the breadcrumbs in a large mixing bowl. Pour over the milk and squish the bread down with the back of a wooden spoon. Leave the bread to soak for 15 minutes, then stir in the sliced speck, salami and garlic.
2. Sprinkle in three-quarters of the chopped chives and crack in the eggs. Stir to incorporate and season with salt and pepper, then add 40g of the grated Parmigiano and spoon in the flour to bind the mixture. Leave the mixture to rest for 15 minutes.
3. Heat the stock in a large 5-litre saucepan and bring to a simmer.

4. Wet your hands to roll the canederli into the size of small satsumas (you should have enough mixture to make 12). If you prefer, use two tablespoons and form beautifully-shaped quenelles.
5. Drop the rolled and formed canederli into the simmering stock and cook over a medium heat for 15–20 minutes – they are ready when they have swollen in size.
6. Remove the canederli with a slotted spoon, place 3 per person into warm bowls with a ladle of the beef stock, and a sprinkle of Parmigiano and chopped chives.

CARMELA'S TIPS:

- I love to shallow-fry the canederli in olive oil until golden, instead of cooking them in stock – they make a great snack – and the cooked canederli freeze incredibly well.
- For a lighter dumpling I often add half a teaspoon of bicarbonate of soda to the mixture when I add the flour.

Bread Pasta and Borlotti Beans,
Pisarei e fasò

The essence of this dish, which hails from the province of Piacenza in the wonderful region of Emilia Romagna, is simplicity. It combines breadcrumbs with flour and water, and is served with beans. What I love about this pasta is the story that comes with it. As this pasta is extruded with the side of your thumb, if you make it frequently enough you may form a firm, hardened spot, like a callus, on your hand. This callus would please any future mother-in-law because not only does it mean you can make pisarei, but also that her little son will not go hungry! I giggle as I write this because it is so whimsical yet I believe every word of it. My, how things have changed. I will now go and place my pan of water on to boil, knowing full-well that my right thumb has the most perfect pasta callus on it. Lucky husband.

Serves: 6
Preparation time: 30 minutes, including resting time
Cooking time: 30 minutes

For the pasta
400g '00' flour
150g very fine, stale breadcrumbs
400ml warm water

For the sauce
2 tbsp extra virgin olive oil
70g lardo (cubed pork fat) or regular lard, chopped then
crushed to make a rough paste
1 large shallot, finely chopped
400g tin of borlotti beans, drained
240g tomato passata
sprig of rosemary, needles finely chopped
1 small Parmigiano rind (optional)
salt and freshly ground black pepper
80g Parmigiano-Reggiano, grated, to serve

1. Tip the flour and breadcrumbs onto a wooden board or a clean work surface and make a well in the centre.
2. Gradually pour in the water and mix to form a dough. Knead until smooth, then cover in cling film and allow to rest at room temperature for 20 minutes.
3. Cut the rested dough into 6 portions. Roll each portion into a long rope, then pinch off bean-sized pieces of dough.
4. Use your thumb to push each piece of pasta away from you, forming a shell. I prefer to make pisarei on a smooth surface rather than using a gnocchetti board but if you prefer, please feel free to use a gnocchetti board and have them *rigate* (ridged).
5. Once all the pisarei are made, cover them with a clean tea towel to prevent them drying out and make your bean sauce.
6. Melt the olive oil and softened lardo in a saucepan over a low heat, add the shallot and cook for about 5 minutes until soft. Add the tinned beans and stir, then pour in the passata. Season with salt and pepper, add the rosemary and the Parmigiano rind (if using). Cook the bean sauce for 20 minutes or so.
7. Bring a large saucepan of water to the boil, then salt it well.
8. Cook the pisarei in the boiling water for 5 minutes, or until al dente. Strain and add the pisarei to the bean sauce. Stir and remove from the heat.
9. Serve the beans and pasta in warm bowls, topped with grated Parmigiano.

Breaded Celery Sticks, *Sedano impanato*

I have a fondness for breading and frying pretty much anything
from my kitchen. It's simple, satisfying, relatively quick, and beyond
easy to eat. Every Italian household would have the basic
ingredients for a soffritto. Celery is a must, and it works perfectly in
this recipe. My son adores celery and this has always been a sure-
fire way to ensure he maintains this love. Plus, we all know that
fried food in moderation is ridiculously indulgent.

Serves: 4 as a snack
Preparation time: 10 minutes
Cooking time: 30 minutes

1 small head of celery, with leaves
2 eggs
150g stale breadcrumbs
2 tbsp polenta
80g Parmigiano-Reggiano, grated, plus extra to serve
light olive oil, for frying
salt and freshly ground black pepper

1. First, prepare your head of celery. Peel each stalk, to remove the
   stringy outer coat and membrane. Cut each stalk into 7cm
   lengths. Retain any celery leaves, finely chop them and place to
   one side (you should have about 1 tablespoon of chopped leaves).
2. Bring a large saucepan of water to the boil. Once boiling, salt it
   well, add the prepared celery stalks and cook for 8–10 minutes
   until tender.
3. Meanwhile, break the eggs into a small, shallow bowl and whisk.
   Season with a little salt and pepper. Put the breadcrumbs,
   polenta, celery leaves and 50g of the Parmigiano in another
   shallow bowl. Stir to incorporate and season well with salt and
   pepper.
4. Heat a few tablespoons of olive oil in a frying pan over a low heat.
5. Drain the celery and allow to cool.
6. Dip each celery stick into the whisked egg and then into the
   breadcrumbs. Repeat as required.

7. Shallow-fry the celery in batches for 8 minutes per batch until golden in colour, turning them in the oil with tongs. Repeat until all the celery has been fried. Place on a platter and serve with the additional grated Parmigiano.

CARMELA'S TIPS:
- Retain the remaining celery leaves and add them to another sugo or stock.
- This recipe also works incredibly well with quartered fennel or sweet carrots.

Egg Spätzle, *Spätzle alle uova*

I wrote about spätzle in my second cookbook, *A Passion for Pasta*. They are referred to as 'sparrows' beaks' due to the way they are extruded over a pan of water. It's a little mesmerising, in all honesty. My spätzle are infused with copious amounts of freshly blanched spinach, which makes them a stunning shade of verdant green. I was told off by someone on social media for adding the leafy veg to the mixture, making them untraditional, so I thought that I would remedy things here with my innocent, leaf-free version. Even though spätzle were born in the mountain climes of Northern Italy, bordering Austria, they really do echo all that is *cucina povera* cooking to me, offering the simplest style and total unfussiness.

Serves: 4
Preparation time: 5 minutes, plus 30 minutes resting time
Cooking time: 10 minutes
You will need: a späztle maker

350g '00' flour
3 eggs
100ml full-fat milk or water
100g salted butter
6 sage leaves
salt and freshly ground black pepper
favourite cheese, for grating, to serve

1. Put the flour in a large bowl, crack in the eggs, add the milk or water and whisk well, until smooth. Season with salt and pepper and stir.
2. Cover the loose dough and leave to rest at room temperature for 30 minutes. The dough will thicken slightly and become glutinous.
3. Bring a large saucepan of water to the boil, then salt it well.
4. Melt the butter in a large, shallow saucepan over a medium heat with a pinch each of salt and pepper. Add the sage leaves and cook for 4 minutes until lightly golden.

5. Place your spätzle maker over the pan of water and spoon in the wet dough. Using a spatula, push the dough firmly through the small holes of the flat spätzle disc.

6. Once the dough has been extruded through the holes of the spätzle maker, add another large spoonful of the dough. Repeat until all of the dough has been used. The spätzle will bob to the top of the pan when ready. They only take a few minutes, but press the entire mixture into the pan before removing any, as the first batch will remain happy bobbing along.

7. Scoop the spätzle out with a slotted spoon and place them directly into the pan of melted butter. Stir well to coat the spätzle and serve in warm bowls with a little cheese of your choice.

CARMELA'S TIP:

- If you do not have a spätzle maker then use an upside-down colander with wide holes or a wide-holed grater.

Filled savoy cabbage, *Cavolo ripieno*

This dish may look a little time-consuming to put together, but in reality it's relatively speedy, reassuringly scrumptious and well worth the effort. I prefer to double up the recipe, as these rolls freeze really well too. The savoy cabbage has a wonderful, almost scale-like texture and is in season from November through to mid-spring.

Serves: 4
Preparation time: 20 minutes
Cooking time: 1 hour
You will need: cocktail sticks

16 savoy cabbage leaves

For the meat filling
2 tbsp extra virgin olive oil
1 shallot, finely chopped
1 garlic clove, finely chopped
200g soft Italian sausages, skinned and meat cut into small pieces
400g veal mince
50ml white wine
300ml chicken or vegetable stock
sprig of rosemary
250g ricotta
40g slightly stale breadcrumbs
70g Parmigiano-Reggiano, grated
4 tbsp chopped parsley
1 egg
salt and freshly ground black pepper

For the tomato sauce
3 tbsp extra virgin olive oil
1 shallot, finely chopped
1 garlic clove, crushed
1 x 680g jar passata
1 tsp dried marjoram
handful of basil leaves

For the topping
50g stale breadcrumbs
50g Parmigiano-Reggiano, grated
1 tsp dried oregano

1. Wash the savoy cabbage leaves then carefully remove the bitter central stem, trying to keep the leaf whole. You will need 16 leaves.

2. Bring a large pan of water to the boil, then salt it. Boil the leaves for 5 minutes, drain on kitchen paper (to remove excess water) and set aside.

3. To make the filling, heat the oil in a large frying pan over a medium heat, add the shallots and garlic and gently soften for 5 minutes.

4. Add the sausage pieces to the pan along with the veal mince and fry for 10 minutes until lightly coloured all over, using the back of a wooden spoon to break up the mince. Add the wine and cook for 5 minutes until the aroma of the wine has evaporated, then pour in the stock, add the rosemary sprig, and season with salt and pepper. Stir and cook for 25 minutes, then remove from the heat and allow to cool a little.

5. While the meat filling is cooking, prepare the simple tomato sauce. Heat the oil in a frying pan over a medium heat, add the shallot and garlic, stir and cook for about 10 minutes until soft and translucent, then pour in the passata and season with salt and pepper. Add the marjoram, stir and cook for 20 minutes, then remove from the heat.

6. Preheat the oven to 180°C fan (400°F/gas 6).

7. Put the ricotta, breadcrumbs, Parmigiano, chopped parsley and egg in a large bowl, stir and spoon in the cooled meat mixture. Stir, taste and season if necessary.

8. Taste and season the tomato sauce and add fresh basil.

9. Add 2 tablespoons of the meat filling mixture to the centre of a cabbage leaf, fold the base and the top inwards then roll it up and secure with a cocktail stick. Repeat with the remaining filling and cabbage leaves.

10. Place the stuffed cabbage leaves in an ovenproof dish and spoon over a little of the tomato sauce. Mix together the topping ingredients and sprinkle them over the cabbage rolls.

11. Bake in the oven for 25 minutes, until bubbling. Remove and serve warm.

CARMELA'S TIP:
- You could use cavolo nero instead of savoy cabbage, however the leaves would need cooking for an additional 10 minutes as they are much firmer in texture.

Fontina fondue, *Fonduta alla valdostana*

Cheese-lovers will truly enjoy this regional, retro and very indulgent cheese fondue recipe. Fontina is a soft cow's milk cheese, nutty and buttery, with a real intensity of flavour, and it is wonderful for melting. It comes from the smallest alpine region of Italy, known as Valle d' Aosta. Fontina has distinctive small holes and bubbles, and has been registered since 1995 and protected by 'Protected Designation of Origin' (PDO).

Serves: 4
Preparation time: 10 minutes, plus 1 hour or overnight steeping
Cooking time: 20 minutes

400g fontina
200ml full-fat milk
35g salted butter
4 egg yolks
freshly ground black pepper

To serve
slices of toasted bread
pre-cooked polenta, sliced

1. Remove the rind of the cheese then place the cheese in 100ml of the milk. and leave it to steep for at least an hour (or overnight) in the fridge.
2. Place a heavy-based saucepan on the hob over a low heat, add the butter and let it slowly melt. Drain the fontina (retaining the milk) and add the fontina to the butter along with the remaining 100ml of milk, topping up (if too dry) as necessary with the retained soaking milk. Let it melt, stirring constantly to ensure no lumps are formed. Add the egg yolks and continue to stir, cooking the mixture for 15–20 minutes until it becomes thick and velvety. Taste and season with pepper.
3. Transfer the cheese to warmed bowls or serve in a 1970s-style fondue (you've probably got one hiding at the back of your kitchen cupboard!).

4. I serve my fonduta with toasted rustic bread or slices of pre-cooked polenta.

CARMELA'S TIP:
*   Retain the egg whites for a pavlova. They freeze perfectly well for up to 3 months.

Fried Stuffed Olives, *Olive all'ascolana*

Time and a little patience are required here. Time I can give, but I have no patience at all. So, I have adapted my recipe to make these morsels of pure unadulterated pleasure totally manageable. The only problem you'll have is that one batch is truly not enough, so double up the quantities. Normally the olives would be peeled carefully so that the entire skin and flesh remains as one piece, you would then take a small ball of filling and reattach the flesh of the olive to form a plump olive, then coat and deep-fry. This requires patience and good knife skills; I have neither so opt to de-stone and fill them instead. If you have an urging to attempt the full-on method then I bow to you and commend you.

Makes: 40–50 stuffed olives
Preparation time: 30 minutes
Cooking time: 20 minutes
You will need: a cherry stoner

400g Castelvetrano olives
light olive oil, for frying
30ml milk
1 egg
250g stale breadcrumbs
½ tsp dried marjoram
70g '00' flour
salt and freshly ground black pepper

For the filling
60g veal mince
60g pork mince
60g beef mince
50g Parmigiano-Reggiano, grated
1 egg yolk
grated zest of 1 small lemon
pinch of freshly grated nutmeg

1. First, prepare the olives. Lightly crush each olive with the side of a knife. Using a cherry stoner, remove the stone and repeat with all the olives. Alternatively, peel each olive as mentioned in the introduction above.
2. Put the veal, pork and beef mince in a bowl and, using a wooden spoon, break up and combine the mince. Add the grated Parmigiano, egg yolk, lemon zest and nutmeg, season with salt and pepper and mix well.
3. Fill and pack each olive with as much of the meat filling as possible. Set aside.
4. Pour the olive oil into a wide saucepan to a depth of 7–8cm (you will need about 300ml) and heat it until it reaches 190°C (375°F). I normally just toss in a little bread – if it sizzles when it hits the oil, you are good to go.
5. Mix the milk and egg in a bowl with a pinch of salt. Place the stale breadcrumbs in a separate bowl with the marjoram, and add the flour to a third bowl and season it with salt and pepper.
6. Dredge the filled olives in the seasoned flour, dip them into the eggy liquid, then roll them in the breadcrumbs.
7. Fry the olives in batches in the hot oil for 4–5 minutes per batch until golden. Remove with a slotted spoon and place on kitchen paper to drain the excess oil.
8. Serve alongside your aperitivo or antipasto.

Hunter's Rabbit, *Coniglio alla cacciatora*

The words 'rabbit season' remind me of both my father Rocco and of the wonderful cartoon character from many moons ago, 'Elmer Fudd' – 'wabbit season!' Growing up on a small farm you can only imagine the fun that was had with the change of each season. Be it rabbit or pheasants, something would always be hanging from the barns – a little gruesome, like a PG-rated scary movie. Rabbit is still not hugely popular here in the UK and isn't as easily available as it is in Italy. That said, search it out, order from your butcher and try my 'Coniglio alla Cacciatore'.

Serves: 4
Preparation time: 20 minutes
Cooking time: 1 hour 45 minutes

900g rabbit pieces, small bones removed if possible
3 tbsp '00' flour, seasoned with salt and pepper
4 tbsp light olive oil
2 shallots, finely chopped
1 celery stick, finely chopped
250g pancetta, cubed
2 garlic cloves, thinly sliced
small bunch of parsley, stalks and leaves separated and finely chopped
250ml white wine or vermouth
small pinch of dried chilli flakes (optional)
200ml chicken stock
400g tin of cherry tomatoes
1 tbsp tomato purée
40g salted capers, rinsed well
sprig of rosemary
1 bay leaf
salt and freshly ground black pepper

To serve
Whipped Milk Polenta (page 140)
1 tbsp chopped celery leaves

1. Dust the rabbit pieces with the seasoned flour and preheat the oven to 180°C fan (400°F/gas 6).
2. Heat 3 tablespoons of the oil in a large casserole dish and fry the rabbit pieces for roughly 15 minutes until coloured all over (in batches if necessary). Once coloured, remove the rabbit from the pan and set aside.
3. Add the remaining oil to the pan along with the shallots, celery and pancetta. Stir and cook over a low heat for 10 minutes. Add the garlic and half of the parsley and fry, stirring, for 2 minutes.
4. Place the rabbit pieces in the base of the pan and add the wine or vermouth. Increase the heat to medium and cook until the wine has reduced by a quarter. Season with salt and pepper and a few chilli flakes (if using). Pour in the chicken stock and stir in the cherry tomatoes, tomato purée, capers, rosemary sprig and bay leaf.
5. Cover and place in the oven for 1 hour. After an hour has passed, taste the sauce for additional seasoning and adjust as required. Add the parsley stalks. Place back in the oven with the lid on for another 20 minutes or so, until the sauce has thickened and the rabbit is perfectly tender. Serve on a bed of whipped polenta and scatter over the parsley leaves and celery leaves.

CARMELA'S TIP:
- I love a salty hit, so just before serving I scatter over a handful of chopped olives.

Mixed Boiled Meats with Vegetables and Mostarda di Cremona, *Bollito misto*

One-pot cooking can serve a family or create an elaborate feast. *Bollito misto* is served across the northern plains of Italy with slight variations, and it is said that if a restaurant has it on the menu then it must be a fine establishment indeed. It takes a little time and patience, but not a great deal of cooking experience as everything is boiled together. Serve with mostarda di frutta (sweet syrup-steeped fruits) and boiled vegetables.

Serves: 6–8
Preparation time: 20 minutes
Cooking time: 4 hours

3 shallots, halved (skin on)
2 garlic cloves, peeled and left whole
1 leek, trimmed, cut into 4cm-thick slices and washed well
2 celery sticks, cut into 4cm chunks
2 carrots, cut into 4cm chunks
1 fennel bulb, quartered
800g beef brisket
5 ripe tomatoes, halved
6 pink peppercorns
small bunch of parsley, leaves and stems separated and chopped
4 ossobuco or cut of veal of your choice
2 bay leaves
1 chicken, jointed
2 tbsp chopped celery leaves
salt and freshly ground black pepper

To serve
extra virgin olive oil
mostarda di frutta (Cremona)

1. Find a large pan and put it on the hob – I'd recommend at least a 7-litre size if you have one to hand. Put the shallots, garlic, leek, celery, carrot and fennel in the pan, fill the pan three-quarters

full with water and bring to the boil. Once boiling, add the beef brisket, halved tomatoes, peppercorns and roughly chopped parsley stems.

2. Cover the pan and cook over a medium heat for 1 hour 20 minutes. Every 15 minutes, lift the lid and skim off and discard any scum that may have risen to the surface.

3. Add the ossobuco and the bay leaves, clamp on the lid and cook for a further hour.

4. Add the jointed chicken pieces and cook for another 1 hour 30 minutes. Season with salt and pepper.

5. Remove from the heat and add the chopped parsley leaves and celery leaves.

6. Once the bollito is ready, take a warm platter, transfer the brisket to the platter, slice it and lay on the platter along with the ossobuco and chicken. Add a ladle of the stock.

7. I take out the boiled veg and serve them in a side dish as they are just delicious mashed onto some bread with a little extra salt.

8. Serve the bollito with a variety of mixed vegetables, mostarda di frutta and good extra virgin olive oil.

9. Drain and retain any leftover stock to make risotto later in the week.

CARMELA'S TIP:
- You can also add a pre-cooked *cotechino* about 45 minutes before serving.

Pasta with a Three-meat Ragù,

Maccheroni alla chitarra con ragù

Much loved, and also hailing from the region of Abruzzo, pasta alla chitarra is similar to a wider, thicker style of linguine. It is made by rolling a sheet of pre-rolled pasta over and through a pasta chitarra. Paired with this classic meat-based ragù this dish will soon become a family favourite. A chitarra is an old-fashioned pasta tool that has strings so that when the pasta is rolled with the firm pressure of a rolling pin it is cut into its desired length and thickness. This is a much-loved tool in my kitchen: you will find a chitarra hanging in most Abruzzi kitchens as well as in my pasta room.

Serves: 4
Preparation time: 30 minutes
Cooking time: 3 hours
You will need: a pasta machine, and a chitarra (optional)

3 tbsp olive oil
1 tbsp Italian lard (strutto)
1 shallot, finely chopped
1 celery stick, finely chopped
1 carrot, finely chopped
2 garlic cloves, crushed
1 small red chilli, deseeded and finely chopped
200g braising beef, cut into small cubes
200g pork shoulder, cut into small cubes
200g lamb neck fillet, cut into small cubes
125ml red wine
500g fresh tomato pulp or passàta
small bunch of basil
80g Pecorino Romano, grated, plus a Pecorino or Parmigiano rind (optional)
400g egg pasta dough (page 165)
50g semola flour, for dusting
salt and freshly ground black pepper

1. First, make the ragù. Heat the oil with the lard in a medium saucepan over a medium heat, add the shallot, celery and carrot and cook for 15 minutes until soft and translucent. Stir in the garlic and chilli, cook for 1 minute, then add all three meats and sear for 10 minutes, letting them colour all over.

2. Pour in the wine and cook for 5 minutes until the wine has evaporated, leaving you with an incredible aroma. Then, add the tomato pulp or passata, 4 of the basil leaves and the optional cheese rind. Season with salt and pepper and cook for 2 hours (uncovered), stirring and checking it intermittently to adjust seasoning. If the sauce begins to dry out, add a little water, stock or mozzarella water to loosen it.

3. Now, make the pasta. Roll the pasta dough out to level-4 thickness on your pasta machine (about the thickness of a 50-pence coin) and cut the pasta sheets into 30cm lengths.

4. Lay a sheet of the cut pasta onto a chitarra and dust the sheet, front and back, with flour. Using a rolling pin, roll the pasta through the fine strings. Repeat until all of the pasta has been cut.

5. If you do not have a chitarra, then simply cut the sheets by hand into thin strips, the width of linguine.

6. Cook the pasta in a large pan of boiling salted water for 4 minutes until al dente.

7. Check the sauce for seasoning, then drain the pasta and dress it with the sauce and half of the grated Pecorino, and the remaining basil as required.

8. Serve on a large, warmed serving platter and sprinkle over the additional Pecorino.

CARMELA'S TIP:
- I sometimes like to leave the meat in whole 200g pieces then, once they are slow-cooked, I tear and shred the meat. If you don't have a pasta machine, then simply roll the dough with a rolling pin, broom handle or wine bottle to the thickness of a 50-pence coin and cut strips using your hands, as mentioned above.

Polenta and Brossa (whey of fontina),
Polenta e brossa

La brossa is a waste product from the production of fontina cheese. Brossa is produced by skimming the whey, which is then added to citric acid and heated. The final brossa, a silky, white-as-snow liquid, is skimmed from the top. There is something almost whimsical when it comes to such an old and classically regional recipe – something almost unknown. It has an essence of purity with an addition of richness. I'm choosing to use quick-cook polenta for speed here, however you can substitute quick-cook for the bramata variety instead if you wish.

Serves: 4
Preparation time: 10 minutes
Cooking time: 15 minutes

> 1.5 litres vegetable stock or water
> 1 tbsp extra virgin olive oil
> 500g quick-cook polenta
> 40g salted butter
> 70g Parmigiano-Reggiano, grated, plus extra to serve
> 1 litre cold brossa (see Tip)
> salt and freshly ground black pepper

1. Heat the stock or water in a large saucepan over a medium heat. Pour in the oil, then slowly add the polenta, stirring constantly with a wooden spoon, and cook for about 8 minutes. If lumps begin to form, swap to using a hand whisk. Season with salt and pepper.
2. Take the polenta off the heat and stir in the butter and Parmigiano. Beat with a wooden spoon and check for additional seasoning.
3. Spoon the polenta into four shallow bowls and ladle the cold brossa around the polenta.
4. Serve with an additional grating of Parmigiano.

CARMELA'S TIPS:
- If no brossa is available, mix together half double cream with half full-fat milk. Season, bring to a simmer for 10 minutes, then leave to cool. Chill in the fridge until required (it will keep for

up to 5 days).

- Add a little grated nutmeg to the finished dish for added flavour, if you like.

Veal Meatloaf with Speck and Boiled Eggs, *Polpettone di vitello e' uva*

This dish hails from the south of Italy but is loved, made, cooked and eaten in all twenty regions, with different twists and additions. Feel free to mix beef, venison or pork mince with the veal for a tweak of flavour. I personally adore veal, so prefer to use it solely as I enjoy a slightly sweeter taste.

Serves: 6
Preparation time: 20 minutes
Cooking time: 1 hour 15 minutes

900g veal mince
2 garlic cloves, crushed
150g stale breadcrumbs
150g Parmigiano-Reggiano, grated
1 egg
½ tsp dried chilli flakes
1 tsp dried oregano
small bunch of parsley, finely chopped (including stems)
12 slices of speck
6 hard-boiled eggs (for the filling)
20 basil leaves
150ml vermouth or dry white wine
salt and freshly ground black pepper

To serve
Whipped Milk Polenta (page 140)
cavolo nero cooked in garlic, chilli and passata

1. Preheat the oven to 190°C fan (410°F/gas 6).
2. Put the veal mince in a large bowl and break it up with a wooden spoon. Tumble in the crushed garlic, stale breadcrumbs, Parmigiano and egg and stir well with a wooden spoon to incorporate. Sprinkle in the chilli flakes, oregano and parsley leaves and stems, season with a good sprinkle of salt and pepper

and mix really well. I prefer to use my hands to mix everything together.

3. Lay a large sheet of baking parchment on a clean board – this will ensure the polpettone mixture will not stick and will aid in rolling. Lay 6 slices of the speck across the parchment and lay 10 basil leaves on top of the speck. Spoon out the meat mixture onto the speck then use your hands to press the meat out to a large 40 x 20cm rectangle, about 3cm deep.

4. Take the other 6 slices of speck and lay them across the flat polpettone mixture. Top with the remaining basil leaves then lay the boiled eggs across the middle of the polpettone rectangle.

5. Gently roll the polpettone (as you would a Swiss roll), using the parchment to guide you, until it is rolled tightly and sealed. Fold in the sides until you have one large sausage shape. Remove the parchment and discard.

6. Lay the polpettone in a large ovenproof dish and add the vermouth or wine. Cover the dish with foil and bake in the oven for 50 minutes, then remove the foil and cook for a further 25 minutes until golden and burnished. Baste with the juices intermittently.

7. Remove from the oven, slice and serve with whipped polenta and cavolo nero.

Roman Oxtail Stew, *Coda alla vaccinara*

A Roman classic that benefits from a long, slow cook, then being reheated and eaten the following day. There are many variations of this dish: sometimes a cinnamon stick is added, or dried fruit, or nutmeg and cocoa powder.... not things you would necessarily consider when thinking of a classical Roman dish. In this version, the celery shines through. *Coda alla vacccinara* showcases the oxtail – a cheap, inexpensive cut referred to as the fifth offal – in an effortless manner. Many years ago, Roman butchers were nicknamed 'tail-eaters' due to the amount of oxtail that they would consume. Stock up on oxtail and make a big batch: this stew is inexpensive, simple in preparation but freezes incredibly well, too.

Serves: 4
Preparation time: 20 minutes
Cooking time: 4 hours 30 minutes

1.5kg oxtail, cut into small pieces (ask your butcher to do this for you, or buy it ready-chopped)
50g '00' flour, seasoned with salt and pepper
30g Italian lard (strutto)
2 tbsp olive oil
250g pancetta or guanciale , diced
1 large shallot, finely chopped
3 celery sticks, 1 finely chopped, 2 cut into 7cm-long pieces
1 carrot, finely chopped
2 garlic cloves, thinly sliced
2 bay leaves
1 cinnamon stick
sprig of rosemary
2 sprigs of thyme
200ml full-bodied red wine
2 tbsp tomato purée
400g tin of pelati (plum) tomatoes, crushed
beef stock, as required
50g raisins
1 tsp cocoa powder

salt and freshly ground black pepper

To serve
soft polenta (see page 140 for my Whipped Milk Polenta recipe)
1 tbsp finely chopped celery leaves
50g untoasted pine nuts

1. Dip the oxtail pieces in the seasoned flour.
2. Heat the oil and lard in a large heavy-based saucepan over a medium heat, add the oxtail and fry (in batches if necessary) for 15 minutes until seared all over. Remove the oxtail from the pan and set aside.
3. Add the pancetta or guanciale to the pan along with the shallot, finely chopped celery stick and carrot and fry over a medium heat for 10 minutes (you need no extra fat at this stage as the pancetta's fat will render down as it cooks).
4. Add the garlic and cook for 1 minute, stirring, then place the oxtail back in the pan and add the bay leaves, cinnamon stick, rosemary and thyme sprigs followed by the wine. Allow the wine to evaporate for a couple of minutes before adding the tomato purée and crushed tomatoes. Add the 7cm lengths of celery and enough beef stock to cover the oxtail completely – the amount of stock you need will depend on the size of your pan. Season with salt and pepper.
5. Cover and cook over a low heat for 4 hours, checking intermittently to taste for seasoning and to see if the sauce requires any more stock.
6. While the oxtail is cooking, soak the raisins in a bowl with a little beef stock for 30 minutes.
7. Once the stew is ready, remove and discard the cinnamon stick and sprigs of herbs if you can find them. Add the cocoa powder and stir.
8. Spoon the stew onto soft polenta, scattering over the celery leaves, drained raisins and pine nuts.

CARMELA'S TIP:
*   I have chosen to serve the oxtail stew with polenta here, but the sauce is incredible served with rigatoni as *rigatoni rigate al sugo di coda.*

Stewed Castelluccio Lentils,
Lenticchie in umido

The best sausage and lentils I have ever had came from the region of Umbria, where these lentils hail from. It was made with the best sausages from Norcina and the most fabulous tiny and delicate lentils from Castelluccio, a small town in the mountains of Umbria. Again, I find, like in many recipes, that the simplistic *cucina povera* style of the south of Italy meets the northern plain incredibly well. Here I give you simply lentils. If you'd like to add sausages to the dish at the beginning of cooking, then brown the sausages and add them to the pan of lentils and cook for 45 minutes.

Serves: 4
Preparation time: 10 minutes, plus overnight soaking
Cooking time: 1 hour 15 minutes

400g Castelluccio lentils
1 bay leaf
2 tbsp extra virgin olive oil
25g salted butter
1 large shallot, thinly sliced
1 celery stick, finely cubed
2 garlic cloves, crushed
250ml vegetable stock
400g tin of pelati (plum) tomatoes
Parmigiano rind (optional)
2 tbsp finely chopped celery leaves
salt and freshly ground black pepper
rustic bread, toasted, to serve

1. Soak the lentils overnight in a bowl of cold water with a bay leaf.
2. The next day, drain and rinse the lentils.
3. Heat the olive oil and butter in a shallow sauté pan over a medium heat, add the shallot and cook for 5 minutes until soft and translucent, then add the celery and garlic and cook for 15 minutes.
4. Pour in the stock and tomatoes, using the back of a wooden

spoon to crush the tomatoes, and stir well. Add the drained lentils, Parmigiano rind (if using) and celery leaves and season with salt and pepper. Cook for 1 hour over a medium heat until the lentils have softened and become plump and full. If the lentils require a little more liquid, add a touch of water or mozzarella water.

5. Serve the stewed lentils with toasted rustic bread that has been kissed with a little oil and a touch of rubbed garlic.

Stuffed Squid, *Calamari ripieno*

Calamari either needs to be cooked quickly, or nice and slow. This beauty from the ocean is a firm favourite in our house, especially when it is thinly sliced and slow-cooked in a tomato sugo for Christmas Eve – the memories and aroma of the night before Christmas always come flooding back to me in an instant when I think of this dish. Stuffed and slow-cooked it is also superb: the firm cavity of the calamari makes a perfect vessel to carry a delicious filling and a simple sauce, too. Once cooked, I like to slice them lengthways in half, drizzle them with a little browned butter and serve them on a bed of rocket with lemon wedges and a few crushed rosemary potatoes.

Serves: 4
Preparation time: 30 minutes
Cooking time: 40 minutes
You will also need: cocktail sticks

8 medium calamari, cleaned (tentacles retained and cut into small pieces)
3 tbsp extra virgin olive oil
1 courgette, grated and strained of any excess liquid
1 garlic clove, crushed
300g stale white breadcrumbs
10 baby plum tomatoes, finely chopped
70g frozen peas, defrosted
½ tsp dried chilli flakes
grated zest and juice of 1 small lemon
45g Parmigiano-Reggiano, grated (optional)
1 egg
small bunch of parsley, finely chopped (including stems)
100ml white wine or vermouth
salt and freshly ground black pepper

1. Heat 1 tablespoon of the oil in a small frying pan over a low heat, add the grated courgette, chopped tentacles and garlic and cook for 5 minutes.

2. Meanwhile, put the breadcrumbs, tomatoes, peas, chilli flakes, lemon zest and juice, Parmigiano, egg and parsley leaves and stems in a bowl.
3. Scrape in the cooked ingredients from the frying pan, stir and season with salt and pepper.
4. Fill the cavity of each calamari with the mixture, leaving 1cm free at the top so you can close them. Secure each stuffed calamari with a cocktail stick in a weaving motion. Alternatively, go for an old-school technique and use a needle and thread.
5. Heat the remaining oil in a shallow, wide frying pan and sear each calamari for 5 minutes.
6. Pour in the white wine or vermouth and cook for 30 minutes over a medium heat, uncovered, until tender.
7. Remove from the heat and serve.

Umbrian Pasta and Sausage,

Pasta alla Norcina

Norcina is a town in the region of Umbria, famous for its pork products and charcuterie. This dish is renowned and loved throughout this hilly region. It is hearty and rich, but not in a cloying way; it just offers a sense of warmth and goodness. Virginal and pure in colour, the sauce is bianco – a white sauce. The northern regions do admire their rich and pure sauces, whereas the south have a fundamental love of the red sauce. This is the beauty of regional cooking in Italy.

Serves: 4
Preparation time: 10 minutes
Cooking time: 30 minutes

4 tbsp extra virgin olive oil
1 garlic clove, peeled and left whole
380g Italian sausages, skins removed and meat roughly chopped
150ml white vermouth or dry white wine
200ml single cream
400g penne or an alternative short pasta
70g Pecorino Romano, grated
salt and freshly ground black pepper

1. Bring a large saucepan of water to the boil, then salt it well.
2. Heat the oil in a small saucepan over a low heat, add the garlic clove and chopped sausage and cook for 10–15 minutes until the meat has browned. Remove the garlic clove and discard.
3. Pour the wine into the pan of sausage meat, stir, and allow it to evaporate.
4. Add the cream to the sausage mixture and stir. Season with salt and pepper and cook over a low heat for 15 minutes.
5. Cook the pasta according to the packet instructions but 2 minutes less, ensuring the pasta remains al dente, with a bite.
6. Drain the pasta and add it to the sauce. Serve with a dusting of Pecorino.

Dolci – Desserts and Biscuits

There is nothing more pleasing than to finish a meal with a light dessert or an indulgent slice of cake or biscotti and caffe. The treats, sweets and biscuits in this chapter showcase more regionality from the north and central regions, paired with a touch of seasonality. You will find delicious recipes from sweet baked late summer peaches paired with amaretto to clementine and Campari sorbet, chiacchiere festival biscuits and custard and pine-nut tart. I could eat the entire chapter all over again!

Prepare and make your dessert ahead of time if you can, in order to save time when you serve your fabulous finale at a dinner party or Sunday family mealtime. I always find these kinds of chapters tricky to write because I can only include a limited number of recipes, which is a little unfair. I say this with a smile on my face, as I tended to be *that* child with her nose pressed firmly against the pastry-shop window, dribbling uncontrollably and thinking of nothing more than filling my tummy. Nowadays I need to control these urges a little more.

Fig, raspberry and vanilla jam preserves the taste of late summer, elderflower panna cotta makes the frugal forager in me feel complete, cherries in grappa can make the most wonderful gift, or try spooning out the boozy ruby cherries and using them to top a decadent cake or scoop of gelato. This chapter is simple, clear, concise and delicious, and will hopefully leave you with an insight into a few of my favourite sweets.

Baked Peaches, *Pesche ripiene*

This dish is Piedmontese in origin. The first bite of a fresh peach at room temperature is a lasting memory to be treasured. The inevitable dribble of juice that cascades down my chin leaves me wanting to eat more. As a child I would refer to a peach as a furry fruit, and my mum would always smile lovingly before passing me one to enjoy. Eating peaches fresh is always best, however baking them in the oven intensifies their natural sweetness. Be warned: one is never enough, so make plenty. You can easily substitute the savoiardi for hard amaretti biscuits and the cinnamon for cocoa powder – a few simple changes will leave you with a completely different dessert.

Serves: 6
Preparation time: 20 minutes
Cooking time: 20 minutes
You will need: a food processor

6 large, ripe peaches
200g savoiardi biscuits
grated zest and juice of 1 small lemon
1 egg yolk
½ tsp ground cinnamon
30g candied fruit
125ml marsala
100ml water
20g butter, for greasing
30g icing sugar, for dusting

1. Preheat the oven to 180°C fan (400°F/gas 6) and lightly grease a suitably sized baking dish with butter (a dish large enough to hold your peach halves).
2. Halve the peaches and remove and discard the stones.
3. Put the savoiardi in a food processor with the lemon zest, egg yolk, cinnamon and candied fruit. Pulse until relatively smooth, but with a little texture.

4. Squeeze the lemon juice into a small bowl and add the marsala and water. Stir.
5. Place the peaches cut side up in the greased baking dish and spoon a tablespoon of the filling into and onto each peach. Once all the peaches are filled, drizzle over the marsala liquid. Bake in the oven for 20 minutes, until tender, basting the peaches with liquid from the baking dish halfway through cooking.
6. Serve the baked peaches dusted with icing sugar. They are equally delicious warm or cold.

CARMELA'S TIP:
- Take 4 room-temperature peaches and slice them, leaving on the skin. Place them in a shallow bowl and pour over a small glass of wine. I prefer dry white wine, but a sweeter wine or prosecco works well, too. Enjoy.

Baked Sweet Risotto Pudding,
Risotto al cioccolato

This recipe is one I make to replicate the old-fashioned school days of a warming chocolate rice pudding, rich and oozing with comfort. It's not overly opulent, but it's certainly easy. My children love this sweet comfort food, and as a speedy midweek pudding it certainly hits the spot. It's not traditional by any stretch of the imagination, but it makes for a reassuringly pleasing alternative to baked risotto.

Serves: 2–4 (depending on portion size)
Preparation time: 5 minutes
Cooking time: 50 minutes

300ml double cream
600ml full-fat milk
200g dark chocolate
50g milk chocolate
1 tbsp Frangelico
200g carnaroli risotto rice
½ tsp ground cinnamon
butter, for greasing

1. Preheat the oven to 140°C fan (325°F/gas 3) and grease an oven dish (about 1.4 litres in capacity) with a little butter.
2. Pour the cream and milk into a medium saucepan, bring to a gentle simmer and add the dark and milk chocolate. Stir until melted, then pour in the delicious Frangelico.
3. Add the risotto rice and cinnamon, stir and ensure the rice is fully coated, then pour it into the greased oven dish. Place in the middle of the oven and bake for 50 minutes.
4. Please ensure that you intermittently (every 10 minutes) open the oven and stir the risotto until al dente as this will ensure you finish with a creamy decadent risotto.
5. Eat at your pleasure.

CARMELA'S TIP:
- You can use a flavoured chocolate for a spin on taste.

Cherries Steeped in Grappa, *Ciliegie al grappa*

Grappa brings back terrible memories for my mother, Solidea. As a child she was playing outside with her siblings and after a while she came running into the family kitchen with an incredible thirst. She opened the fridge door and pulled out a small bottle of clear liquid from the bottom of the fridge. Thinking it was water, she took two huge gulps, before immediately realising it was Nonno Angelo's neat grappa that he would keep cool in the fridge. Well, you can only imagine her tiny face at the time. Alcohol has never touched her lips since. Grappa is a very strong, Italian, grape-based 50%-proof alcohol, so it is perfect for steeping and storing fruit for the larder, such as plump, vibrant ruby cherries preserved in advance for a celebration: what could be more perfect!

Makes: 2–3 jars
Preparation time: 10 minutes, plus 2 months' steeping time
You will need: 2–3 sterilised jars (see page 9 for sterilising instructions)

1kg cherries, washed
1 litre grappa
300g granulated sugar

1. Snip off the majority of the cherry stalks but leave a little on for an easy grab opportunity. Using a needle, pierce three holes in each cherry.
2. Place the cherries in 2 or 3 sterilised jars of your choice.
3. Pour the grappa into a large jug and add the sugar. Stir well.
4. Pour the grappa and sugar mixture over the cherries and seal the jars.
5. Allow the cherries to steep for 2 months or so in a cool, dark place.
6. Serve by spooning the doused cherries over a gelato of your choice, then follow with some cherry-infused grappa from the jar, poured over ice. This is for the mouths of adults only.

Chestnut Cake, *Castagnaccio*

From Lucca with love. This is a classic chestnut cake from the region of Tuscany which holds some truly wonderful memories for me, of annual visits to this charming region and the walled city. It's a simple recipe, finished with a scattering of fresh rosemary leaves, soaked raisins, pine nuts and a little olive oil, added just before baking.

Serves: 6
Preparation time: 10 minutes
Cooking time: 25–30 minutes
You will need: a 22cm round cake tin

60g raisins
380ml tepid water
260g chestnut flour
50ml olive oil
35g pine nuts
10 fresh rosemary needles

1. Preheat the oven to 190°C fan (410°F/gas 6). Grease the cake tin and line it with baking parchment.
2. Soak the raisins in a little warm water to plump up for around 10 minutes or so. (For a cheeky alternative, I sometimes soak them in a little amaretto or marsala.)
3. Put the chestnut flour in a large mixing bowl then slowly add the water, whisking as you go to prevent lumps forming. Add 30ml of the olive oil and whisk to combine, then pour the mixture into your prepared cake tin.
4. Drain the raisins and scatter them over the cake mixture, then rinse the pine nuts under a little cold water (this prevents them scorching) and scatter them over the mixture, along with the rosemary needles.
5. Drizzle over the remaining oil and bake in the oven for 25–30 minutes until firm-ish to the touch. Remove from the oven and leave to cool in the tin, then transfer to a wire rack.
6. Slice and eat just as it is but I love to enjoy mine with a little whipped mascarpone.

Clementine and Campari Sorbet,
Sorbetto di clementine e Campari

Clementine and Campari are two of my favourite flavours. The sweetness and aroma of clementine reminds me of Christmas and the bitter ruby tones of Campari whisper in my ear, 'Carmela, please transform me into a Negroni *subito*!' But, for this treat, let's put my own wants and desires to one side, and make this incredibly refreshing and palate-cleansing sorbet.

Serves: 6
Preparation time: 20 minutes
Cooking time: 5 minutes
Freezing time: 4–5 hours

130g caster sugar
550ml clementine juice
100g liquid glucose
4 tbsp Campari
juice of 1 lemon

1. Put the caster sugar in a small saucepan with the clementine juice. Bring to a simmer over a medium heat and stir until the sugar has fully dissolved, then add the liquid glucose and stir for one minute. Remove from the heat and pour in the Campari and lemon juice.
2. Stir and pour into a clean, cold bowl. Transfer the bowl to the freezer for about 2 hours.
3. Use a fork to stir the sorbet mixture well and refreeze, and repeat this process every hour until the sorbet has a smooth yet textured consistency.
4. Refreeze until required.

CARMELA'S TIP:
- Alcohol speeds up the melting process of the sorbet, so please do not add additional Campari.

Custard Tart, *Torta della Nonna*

Another sweet Sunday treat brought to you from the central region of Tuscany (Toscana). Now, whether the tart truly holds its heart in the capital city of Florence or Arezzo, I don't honestly mind, though I personally believe Florence has the historical rights. It makes a wonderful centrepiece at any table, with its golden studded pine nuts, lemon-infused pastry and an amber hue of custard. It's delicious warm or cold!

Serves: 8
Preparation time: 40 minutes plus 1 hour chilling time
Cooking time: 45 minutes
You will need: a 25cm circular fluted flan dish (about 3cm deep)

50g untoasted pine nuts
vanilla icing sugar, for dusting

For the pastry
300g '00' flour
1 tsp baking powder
125g caster sugar
120g chilled salted butter, diced
1 tsp vanilla extract
1 large egg plus 2 large egg yolks
grated zest of ½ lemon

For the custard
500ml full-fat milk
grated zest of 1 small lemon
2 large eggs
140g caster sugar
1 tsp vanilla extract or seeds scraped from 1 vanilla pod
30g '00' flour, plus extra for dusting

1. First, make the pastry. Put the flour, baking powder, sugar and butter into a bowl. Using the tips of your fingers rub the mixture together until it has a consistency that resembles breadcrumbs.

Add the vanilla and crack in the egg followed by the egg yolks and lemon zest. Bring all of the ingredients together to form a ball of dough, flatten it out into a disc and wrap in cling film. Place in the fridge for at least 1 hour to chill.

2. Preheat the oven to 180°C fan (400°F/gas 6).

3. While the pastry is chilling, make the custard. Bring the milk to a simmer in a heavy-based saucepan and add the lemon zest.

4. Crack the eggs into a heatproof bowl and add the sugar, vanilla and flour. Whisk to combine.

5. Slowly add the warmed milk to the egg mixture, whisking continuously, then return the mixture to the pan and heat gently for 5 minutes until thickened. Please be careful to not overheat the mixture, as the custard may catch at the bottom of the pan.

6. Once thickened, remove from the heat and allow the mixture to cool.

7. Remove the pastry from the fridge. Take two-thirds of the pastry and roll it out on a lightly floured surface to a thin disc about 3mm thick. Line the base and sides of your flan dish with the pastry, using your fingers to push the pastry into all the crevices. Use a fork to pierce the base of the pastry several times.

8. Pour the cooled custard into the pastry shell and level it out.

9. Roll the remaining pastry to make another 3mm-thick disc and lay it on top of the flan, use your fingertips or a fork to seal around the edges of the pastry case and cut off any overhang. To ensure the pine nuts do not burn, run them under cold water, then sprinkle them over the tart.

10. Bake the tart in the oven for 45 minutes until slightly golden and speckled with colour. Remove from the oven and allow it to cool fully before removing it from the dish. Sprinkle with a generous amount of vanilla icing sugar and serve.

Elderflower Panna Cotta, *Panna cotta*

Here, early summer elderflowers, foraged from the stunning fields of the UK, infuse one of the most classic desserts from the Piedmontese region of Italy. Elderflower has a delicate aroma with stunningly beautiful, tiny white flowers, which are high on the list of the most popular wild flowers that are foraged when in season. Once picked, they are best used within a few hours.

Serves: 6
Preparation time: 30 minutes
Cooking time: 10 minutes
Chilling time: 2 hours

5 gelatine leaves
500ml full-fat milk
400ml double cream
seeds scraped from 1 vanilla pod (keep the pod)
90g granulated sugar
12 fresh elderflower heads
6 biscotti, to serve

1. Soak the gelatine leaves in a bowl of cold water for 10 minutes until floppy.
2. Pour the milk and cream into a saucepan, add the seeds from the vanilla pod and the empty vanilla pod, along with the sugar. Scatter in the fresh elderflower heads.
3. Place over a low heat for 10 minutes, stirring gently. Once bubbling, remove from the heat.
4. Strain the cream mixture through a sieve into a clean heatproof bowl or jug and discard the vanilla pod and elderflower heads.
5. Squeeze the excess water from the gelatine leaves and add them immediately to the warm cream mixture. Stir until dissolved.
6. Pour the mixture into 6 martini glasses, cover and chill for 2 hours until set.
7. Serve with biscotti.

Fig, Raspberry and Vanilla Jam,
Fichi e lamponi marmellata

This wonderful jam uses the last of the summer fruits. It is sweet, intensely fruity and has an amazing fullness to it, too. The sweet vanilla adds the most delicate punch and works so well with the plump, voluptuous figs and bright pink raspberries. This has become my favourite jam recipe. I don't think there is anything more comforting than opening a jar of homemade jam and spreading it generously over a chunk of toasted bread. I love the idea of having a cupboard filled with jams, jellies and chutneys as we head towards the depths of winter.

Makes: 3 small jars
Preparation time: 5 minutes
Cooking time: 10 minutes
You will need: 3 small sterilised jam jars (see page 9 for sterilising instructions)

400g fresh ripe figs
350g raspberries
grated zest of 1 small lemon and juice of ½
450g granulated sugar
seeds scraped from 2 vanilla pods (keep the pods)

1. Peel the skins off the figs and retain the entire pulp. Roughly chop the figs and place in a heavy-based saucepan. Tumble in the raspberries and add the lemon zest and juice. Cook over a medium heat for 5 minutes until the raspberries and figs have softened.
2. Add the sugar, stir and cook rapidly over a medium heat for 10 minutes, being careful not to burn the jam, then add the vanilla seeds and the fragrant empty pods to the pan and cook, stirring, for 2 minutes.

3. Check the jam has reached setting point. I do this by placing a small saucer in the freezer for 10 minutes and then, when I think the jam is ready, spooning a teaspoon of the jam onto the cold saucer. Push the jam with the tip of your finger. If it wrinkles, then the jam is set and ready.
4. Remove the vanilla pods and discard.
5. Pour the jam into your sterilised jars and seal tightly. Label and store. The jam will easily keep for up to a year.

Fried Festival Biscuits, *Chiacchiere*

Chiacchiere hold such a special place in my heart. Growing up, my sister and I would refer to them as Mum's fried biscuits. In fact, they are thin strips of sweetened pasta dough that are fried until lightly golden and dusted with vanilla icing sugar. My mum would pile them up in a huge bowl and place them on the dinner table and they'd last a matter of hours at most. These *chiacchiere* are not just for special occasions, they are for any day of the week. When making *chiacchiere* I use a stand mixer with a beater attachment, however, if you prefer, you can use a wooden board and make the sweet dough volcano-style, as you would a standard pasta dough.

Makes: 25 biscuits
Preparation time: 20 minutes, plus 1 hour resting time
Cooking time: 15 minutes
You will need: a frilled pasta cutter, a stand mixer and pasta machine (optional)

60g salted butter, softened
60g caster sugar
1 egg
340g '00' flour, plus extra for dusting
1 tsp vanilla extract or the seeds scraped from 1 vanilla pod
80ml white wine
2 tbsp grappa
1 litre vegetable oil
vanilla icing sugar, for dusting

1. Put the softened butter, sugar and egg in the bowl of a stand mixer fitted with the beater attachment and add 2 tablespoons of the flour. Turn on the mixer and gradually spoon in the remaining flour, along with the vanilla, wine and grappa. Continue to mix until the mixture forms a dough, adding a little more flour if required. Alternatively, to make the dough by hand, place the flour on a clean work surface and make a well in the centre. Add the sugar, butter and egg. Combine with your fingertips, using a light touch, then add the vanilla, wine and

grappa. Carefully form the mixture into a dough.

2. Knead the dough on a lightly floured surface for about 3 minutes, wrap it in cling film and allow it to rest in the fridge for 1 hour.

3. Roll the sweet pasta dough into sheets (level 5 thickness on your pasta machine) using either a rolling pin, broom handle, wine bottle or a pasta machine – whichever you prefer. Ensure the dough has been floured well on both sides as sweet pasta has a softer texture than standard egg-dough pasta. If you are using a rolling pin, roll it to the thickness of a 50-pence piece.

4. Once the pasta dough has been rolled, use a frilled cutter to cut the pasta sheets into strips about 15 x 3cm.

5. Heat the oil in a large high-sided saucepan to 190°C (375°F).

6. Test the oil is hot enough with an offcut of the pasta. If it sizzles immediately, it's ready.

7. Gently lay some pasta strips into the hot oil, placing them away from you. They will puff up instantly. Cook them for 2 minutes, until lightly golden on one side, then flip them over and cook for another 2 minutes. Remove with a slotted spoon, drain on kitchen paper and dust with vanilla icing sugar.

Ladyfinger Biscuits, *Savoiardi*

I remember when I used to visit Nonna Carmela as a little girl she would always make me a cup of weak tea and open a packet of savoiardi biscuits. She would place them delicately onto a plate and serve them to me with a teaspoon. I would sit bent-kneed at the coffee table, waiting patiently. The teaspoon is an essential tool because the savoiardi are so delicate that if they so much as approach a mug of tea they break into an excitable mess. Nowadays, when time allows, I love to make them. They are quick, easy and inexpensive to make, and the fact that they keep in an airtight container for up to 2 weeks is welcome news.

Makes: 40 biscuits
Preparation time: 15 minutes
Cooking time: 12–15 minutes
You will need: a piping bag with a plain round nozzle

6 eggs, separated
150g caster sugar
150g '00' flour
30g vanilla icing sugar, for dusting

1. Preheat the oven to 180°C fan (400°F/gas 6), grease two baking trays and line them with baking parchment.
2. Beat the egg whites in a large, clean mixing bowl using an electric whisk. Once air bubbles form, add the caster sugar, a spoonful at a time.
3. Beat the yolks in a separate bowl until light and pale.
4. Add the beaten yolks to the whites and gently combine, then fold in the flour.
5. Place the mixture in a large piping bag with a plain nozzle and pipe 10cm-long sausages on the lined baking trays (you should have enough mixture for 40 ladyfingers).
6. Bake in the oven for 12–15 minutes until pale golden in colour. Remove from the oven, allow to cool on a wire rack and dust with the icing sugar.

Panforte, *Panforte di Siena*

When I think of panforte, I hear the sound of distant jingle bells and imminent festive joy. It hails from Tuscany, specifically the breathtakingly beautiful city of Sienna. Panforte is rich in flavour, decadent in colour and lightly spiced.

Serves: 8
Preparation time: 10 minutes
Cooking time: 40 minutes
You will need: a small 22 x 22cm baking tin, base and sides lined with baking parchment or edible rice paper.

150g caster sugar
150g honey
35g salted butter
150g blanched almonds
75g blanched hazelnuts
75g shelled pistachios
80g dried figs, roughly chopped
80g candied orange and lemon, thinly sliced
splash of vin santo (fortified sweet wine)
75g '00' flour or plain flour
50g cocoa powder
¼ tsp ground cloves
½ tsp ground cinnamon
½ tsp freshly grated nutmeg
icing sugar, for sprinkling

1. Preheat the oven to 150°C fan (325°F/gas 3).
2. Put the sugar, honey and butter in a saucepan over a low heat and melt gently, using a wooden spoon to stir.
3. Mix the whole nuts, chopped dried figs, sliced candied fruit and vin santo in a large mixing bowl and stir well.
4. Sift the flour and cocoa powder into the bowl of nuts and fruit, stir, then spoon the spices into the bowl, stirring to incorporate fully.

5. Slowly add the melted liquid ingredients to the dry ingredients and stir until well combined.
6. Pour the mixture into the lined tin and level out. Bake in the oven for 40 minutes.
7. Remove from the oven, allow to cool a little, then transfer to a wire rack. The panforte will firm up as it cools. Sprinkle with icing sugar, slice and enjoy with espresso.

CARMELA'S TIP:
- The panforte will keep for up to 2 weeks in a sealed container.

Raspberry Sorbet with Grappa, *Sorbetto di lampone e grappa*

Summer is here. Berries are now in season and their sweetness, aroma and intense colour is at its best. Sorbet has to be the highlight of many a summer evening soirée. Sweet, with a slight sourness, it is the most refreshing after-dinner treat there is, and it's also perfect as a mid-course palate cleanser. Grappa is my fluid of choice here but equally, sambuca or vodka would marry beautifully.

Serves: 4
Preparation time: 5 minutes
Cooking time: 15 minutes
Chilling time: 2–3 hours

250ml water
250g granulated sugar
1kg raspberries, crushed
grated zest and juice of 1 lemon
60ml grappa
mint leaves, to garnish

1. Put the water and sugar in a saucepan over a medium heat and allow the sugar to dissolve for 4 minutes.
2. Once the sugar has dissolved, tumble in the crushed raspberries and cook over a medium heat for 5 minutes.
3. Remove from the heat and set aside for 5 minutes, then add the lemon zest and juice and stir. Add the grappa and taste, adjusting the sweetness or sourness with lemon or sugar as necessary.
4. Place the mixture in a container and pop it in the freezer.
5. Every 30 minutes, use a fork to whisk up the mixture. Place it back in the freezer and repeat this process for 2–3 hours until the sorbet's texture is almost scoopable.
6. Serve in small glasses, garnish with mint leaves.

CARMELA'S TIP:
- The sorbet will only keep in the freezer for 2 days – after that length of time it will become crystallised – so enjoy it while it's fresh.

Semifreddo with Nougat and Melted Chocolate Sauce, *Semifreddo al torrone*

Torrone is a type of Italian nougat that is available in a soft, pliable bar and also in a hard form. Torrone is said to have a long and complicated past, but in terms of regionality it sits very proudly in the city of Cremona in the heart of Lombardy. Torrone makes a celebration complete: any festivities in my home would be a failure if torrone wasn't chopped up and placed on wooden boards. It is so sweet, but it seems to draw you in, ensuring every little bit gets polished up and eaten. I love the classic style, with just almonds and sugar paper, and I absolutely adore the firm dark chocolate blanket that surrounds some torrone – these are a favourite of my father Rocco, too. This dessert deserves to be made at any time, not just for celebrations and Christmas.

Serves: 8–10
Preparation time: 10 minutes
Freezing time: at least 6 hours
You will need: a food processor and a 900g loaf tin (or a similar size mould)

2 large eggs
150g caster sugar
pinch of salt
600ml double cream
400g torrone – the flavour of your choice
1 tsp orange extract
150g dark chocolate
150g milk chocolate

1. Separate the eggs into two clean bowls and line the loaf tin with cling film, ensuring some cling film hangs over the edges as this will help you de-mould the dessert.
2. Add the sugar and pinch of salt to the yolks and whisk for about 3 minutes until pale in colour.
3. Pour the cream into the egg yolk mixture and whisk to fully incorporate and thicken.

4. Put the torrone in a food processor and pulse for 1 minute until it's broken into uneven chunks.
5. Clean the whisk thoroughly, then whisk the whites until they have doubled in size and are light and fluffy, with a moderate firmness.
6. Tumble the torrone into the cream mixture and stir. Spoon in the orange extract.
7. Add the egg whites into the cream mixture a spoonful at a time, folding them in until all the whites have been incorporated.
8. Pour the mixture into the lined loaf tin, cover with cling film and freeze for at least 6 hours.
9. Just before serving, melt both the chocolates in a bain-marie (a small heatproof bowl set over a saucepan of hot water), stirring.
10. Slice the semifreddo, plate up and pour a little melted chocolate over each serving.

CARMELA'S TIP:
- The semifreddo is best consumed from the freezer within 4 days.

Sweet Focaccia, *Focaccia dolce*

A torn piece of this focaccia dipped into a little vin santo, Asti or warmed jam is what sweet dreams are made of. I have few words for this recipe, as I am far too busy salivating and finishing off my second helping of the day. This focaccia makes a perfect base for a sweet treat – my children love it with a generous dollop of chocolate cream or lemon curd. *Buono!*

Makes: 6–8 rounds
Preparation time: 15 minutes (no resting necessary)
Cooking time: about 20 minutes

300g '00' flour
150g caster sugar
5g Maldon sea salt
2 tsp baking powder
1 egg
140g salted butter, melted and cooled, plus extra for greasing
grated zest of 1 lemon
icing sugar, for dusting

1. Preheat the oven to 180°C fan (400°F/gas 6) and grease a baking sheet with a little butter.
2. Put the flour, sugar, salt and baking powder in a bowl and stir.
3. Crack the egg into a bowl and whisk by hand for 2 minutes until pale in colour.
4. Make a well in the centre of the dry ingredients and add the melted butter, egg and lemon zest. Mix gently to incorporate and form a dough – do not over-knead as this will toughen the dough.
5. Portion the dough into 8 equal balls, then roll each ball out into rounds the thickness of a pound coin. Place on the greased baking sheet.
6. Bake in the oven for 15–18 minutes until golden, then remove from the oven and place on a wire rack to cool.
7. Dust with icing sugar and enjoy just as they are, with an early morning espresso.

Tegole Biscotti from Valle d'Aosta,

Valdostana Tegole

This sweet treat celebrates the region of Valle d'Aosta perfectly. Made of ground nuts paired with store-cupboard ingredients, they resemble delicate tuile-like biscuits and take just a few minutes to prepare. Serve them at any time of the day – paired with a strong espresso or small glass of marsala they are incredibly moreish.

Makes: 20 biscotti
Preparation time: 10 minutes, plus minimum 1 hour chilling time
Cooking time: 7–8 minutes

4 egg whites
200g caster sugar
1 tsp vanilla extract
85g ground hazelnuts
85g ground almonds
65g '00' flour, plus extra for dusting
65g salted butter, softened

1. Put the egg whites in a clean mixing bowl. Add the caster sugar and vanilla and whisk well for 2 minutes until aerated. Scatter in the ground nuts and the flour, incorporate gently, then add the softened butter and mix to form a dough. Dust the dough lightly with a little flour. Wrap the dough in cling film and place in the fridge to chill for at least 1 hour (or up to 2 days).
2. Preheat the oven to 180°C fan (400°F/gas 6) and line a baking sheet with baking parchment.
3. Lightly dust a work surface with flour and roll the chilled dough out into 20 x 5cm discs, the thickness of a 5-pence piece.
4. Place the discs on the lined baking sheet and bake in the oven for 7–8 minutes until lightly golden.
5. Remove from the oven. Leave to cool on the baking sheet and transfer to a wire rack once they've hardened a little.

CARMELA'S TIP:
* Retain the egg yolks and make a classic carbonara.

Vanilla Pizzelles, *Pizzelles*

I'm not sure why, but I only tend to make pizzelle at festival times of the year, particularly during Easter and Christmas. They are a wonderful, embossed, almost waffle-like treat made with flour, egg, sugar and oil. Traditionally, anise is added but I often use vanilla and lemon, or clementine zest and juice. They are made with a special embossed waffle iron that sits on the gas hob as you ladle in the mixture, then you press them until golden, and dust with icing sugar. See how many you can enjoy in one go!

Makes: 20 pizzelle
Preparation time: 5 minutes
Cooking time: 20 minutes
You will need: a pizzelle iron or electric pizzelle maker

olive oil, for greasing
3 eggs
200g caster sugar
2 tsp vanilla extract
220g salted butter, melted and cooled
400g '00' flour
2 tsp baking powder
2 tbsp icing sugar, for dusting

1. Preheat the pizzelle iron or turn on the electric pizzelle maker. It may take a good 10 minutes to heat up. Rub it with a little olive oil.
2. Beat the eggs and sugar in a bowl. Add the vanilla and melted butter, then beat again with a wooden spoon. Mix the flour and baking powder together. Gradually add the flour to the wet ingredients until you have a smooth batter.
3. Add 2 tablespoons of the mixture to the pizzelle iron/maker, close the lid and cook for 1 minute until lightly golden. Remove and transfer to a sheet of baking parchment.
4. Repeat making the pizzelles until you've used all the batter, placing each pizelle on a separate sheet of baking parchment.
5. Once cooked and cooled, you can stack them and sprinkle them liberally with icing sugar.

Online stockists

Below I have listed a few of my favourite online stockists for Italian produce and fresh fruit and vegetables.

For food
www.latriestina.co.uk
I adore their guanciale

www.melburryandappleton.co.uk
Great for general Italian larder ingredients

www.vorrei.co.uk
Stock a wonderful range of larder goods

www.natoora.co.uk
Amazing fresh fruit and vegetables

www.seedsofitaly.com
Grow-your-own seeds and deli goods

www.tenutamarmorelle.com
I love their long-stemmed Roman artichokes

www.mydelibox.com
Great range of Italian brands

For pasta tools
www.marcato.it
For the best pasta machines and high-quality pasta attachments and tools. All 100% Italian-made.

www.romagnolipastatools.com
Beautifully crafted corzetti stamps and rolling pins from Tuscany.

Acknowledgements

I really did enjoy writing this, my third Italian cookery book; I think more so than both *Southern Italian Family Cooking* and *A Passion for Pasta*, possibly because over the years I have been cooking and developing these recipes at my fortnightly supper clubs, at my UK-wide cookery classes and at my own family table, so now I finally feel comfortable to share them with you. Tried, tested and loved.

Heritage and family play a massive part in my day-to-day life, influencing how and what I cook, teach and write.

I couldn't have written *Northern and Central Italian Family Cooking* without the support of my immediate family, my children Rocco, Natalia, Santino and Chiara, and not forgetting my husband James, whose tummy benefits greatly from all the good and sometimes experimental dishes I produce. So, thank you from the bottom of my heart. I take constant inspiration from my Italian heritage, old and new. I have learned and continue to learn with love from the lady who is the matriarch of my family, my little Nonna Carmela. So, please enjoy this third treasure of mine and if you are on social media, feel free to follow me across my channels for continued inspiration, posts and videos. Now it's time to write book number four!

Baci Carmela x

Instagram: @carmelaskitchen @my_italian_kitchen_
Twitter: @Carmela_kitchen & @PastaCarmela
Facebook: @Carmelaskitchen
Website: www.carmelas-kitchen.com

Index